AF765067

HEALTH CARE ISSUES, COSTS AND ACCESS

MEDICAID, CHILDREN'S HEALTH INSURANCE AND THE PATIENT PROTECTION AND AFFORDABLE CARE ACT

HEALTH CARE ISSUES, COSTS AND ACCESS

Additional books in this series can be found on Nova's website
under the Series tab.

Additional E-books in this series can be found on Nova's website
under the E-books tab.

HEALTH CARE ISSUES, COSTS AND ACCESS

MEDICAID, CHILDREN'S HEALTH INSURANCE AND THE PATIENT PROTECTION AND AFFORDABLE CARE ACT

ARTHUR T. DUPONT
AND
SARAH L. PEETERS
EDITORS

Nova Science Publishers, Inc.
New York

Copyright © 2011 by Nova Science Publishers, Inc.

All rights reserved. No part of this book may be reproduced, stored in a retrieval system or transmitted in any form or by any means: electronic, electrostatic, magnetic, tape, mechanical photocopying, recording or otherwise without the written permission of the Publisher.

For permission to use material from this book please contact us:
Telephone 631-231-7269; Fax 631-231-8175
Web Site: http://www.novapublishers.com

NOTICE TO THE READER

The Publisher has taken reasonable care in the preparation of this book, but makes no expressed or implied warranty of any kind and assumes no responsibility for any errors or omissions. No liability is assumed for incidental or consequential damages in connection with or arising out of information contained in this book. The Publisher shall not be liable for any special, consequential, or exemplary damages resulting, in whole or in part, from the readers' use of, or reliance upon, this material. Any parts of this book based on government reports are so indicated and copyright is claimed for those parts to the extent applicable to compilations of such works.

Independent verification should be sought for any data, advice or recommendations contained in this book. In addition, no responsibility is assumed by the publisher for any injury and/or damage to persons or property arising from any methods, products, instructions, ideas or otherwise contained in this publication.

This publication is designed to provide accurate and authoritative information with regard to the subject matter covered herein. It is sold with the clear understanding that the Publisher is not engaged in rendering legal or any other professional services. If legal or any other expert assistance is required, the services of a competent person should be sought. FROM A DECLARATION OF PARTICIPANTS JOINTLY ADOPTED BY A COMMITTEE OF THE AMERICAN BAR ASSOCIATION AND A COMMITTEE OF PUBLISHERS.

Additional color graphics may be available in the e-book version of this book.

Library of Congress Cataloging-in-Publication Data

Medicaid, children's health insurance, and the Patient Protection and
Affordable Care Act / editors, Arthur T. Dupont and Sarah L. Peeters.
p. ; cm.
Includes index.
ISBN 978-1-61122-903-5 (hardcover)
1. Medicaid. 2. United States. Patient Protection and Affordable Care
Act. 3. Children's Health Insurance Program (U.S) I. Dupont, Arthur T. II.
Peeters, Sarah L.
[DNLM: 1. United States. Patient Protection and Affordable Care Act. 2.
Children's Health Insurance Program (U.S) 3. Medicaid. 4. Insurance,
Health--United States. 5. Legislation, Medical--United States. W 250 AA1]
RA412.4.M427 2010
368.4'200973--dc22
2010044733

Published by Nova Science Publishers, Inc. † New York

Contents

Preface

The Health Care Reform Law makes many significant changes to the private and public markets for health insurance, as well as modifications to aspects of the publicly financed health care delivery system. It represents the most significant reform to the Medicaid program since its establishment in 1965. This new and important book details some of the major changes to the Medicaid and CHIP programs and provides a timeline of effective dates for these provisions.

Chapter 1- On March 23, 2010, the President signed into law H.R. 3590, the Patient Protection and Affordable Care Act (PPACA, P.L. 111-148), as passed by the Senate on December 24, 2009, and the House on March 21, 2010. PPACA will, among other changes, modify Medicaid and the Children's Health Insurance Program (CHIP) statutes. In addition, on March 21, 2010, the House passed an amendment in the nature of a substitute to H.R. 4872, the Health Care and Education Reconciliation Act of 2010 (HCERA, P.L. 111-152). After being passed by the House, HCERA was subsequently amended and passed by the Senate before being approved again by the House on March 25, 2010. HCERA was signed by the President on March 30, 2010. HCERA, which amends PPACA, combined with PPACA form the health care reform law.

Chapter 2- The President signed into law H.R. 3590, the Patient Protection and Affordable Care Act (PPACA; P.L. 111-148), on March 23, 2010. Seven days later, a second bill, H.R. 4872, was signed into law by the President to modify PPACA. This second law, the Health Care and Education Reconciliation Act of 2010 (HCERA; P.L. 111-152), was signed into law on March 30, 2010. Together these measures constitute what is referred to as the health care reform law, which makes many significant changes to the private and public markets for health insurance, as well as modifies aspects of the publicly financed health care delivery system. It represents the most significant reform to the Medicaid program since its establishment in 1965. This report details some of the major changes to the Medicaid and CHIP programs and provides a timeline of effective dates for these provisions.

In: Medicaid, Children's Health Insurance... ISBN: 978-1-61122-903-5
Editors: A. T. Dupont and S. L. Peeters © 2011 Nova Science Publishers, Inc.

Chapter 1

Medicaid and CHIP: Changes Made by the Health Care and Education Reconciliation Act of 2010 (HCERA, P.L. 111-152) to the Patient Protection and Affordable Care Act (PPACA), P.L. 111-148)*

Evelyne P. Baumrucker, Cliff Binder, Julie Stone and Elicia J. Herz

Summary

On March 23, 2010, the President signed into law H.R. 3590, the Patient Protection and Affordable Care Act (PPACA, P.L. 111-148), as passed by the Senate on December 24, 2009, and the House on March 21, 2010. PPACA will, among other changes, modify Medicaid and the Children's Health Insurance Program (CHIP) statutes. In addition, on March 21, 2010, the House

* This is an edited, reformatted and augmented edition of a United States Congressional Research Service publication, Report R41125, dated April 1, 2010.

passed an amendment in the nature of a substitute to H.R. 4872, the Health Care and Education Reconciliation Act of 2010 (HCERA, P.L. 111-152). After being passed by the House, HCERA was subsequently amended and passed by the Senate before being approved again by the House on March 25, 2010. HCERA was signed by the President on March 30, 2010. HCERA, which amends PPACA, combined with PPACA form the health care reform law.

HCERA includes the following two titles: (1) Coverage, Medicare, Medicaid, and Revenues, and (2) Education and Health. Title I contains provisions related to health care and revenues, including modifications made by HCERA to PPACA. Title II includes amendments to the Higher Education Act of 1965, which authorizes most of the federal programs involving postsecondary education, and other health amendments, which include other changes to PPACA.

This report provides a brief summary of PPACA followed by a discussion of the modifications made to the Medicaid and CHIP provisions by HCERA. This report reflects legislative language in HCERA as passed by the House on March 25, 2010. Selected highlights of the Medicaid and CHIP amendments made by HCERA to PPACA include the following:

- primary care physician payment rates for selected patient treatments were increased;
- the definition of the average manufacturer price (AMP) was revised to help make AMP more closely reflect manufacturers' average prices;
- the effective date of the Community First Choice Option was delayed;
- state FMAP rates for newly eligible populations were changed, as were income counting rules for certain populations;
- the territories' spending rate caps were increased beginning with the second quarter of FY2011;
- additional program integrity funding was provided through indexing of the Medicaid Integrity Program for fiscal years beginning with FY2010; and
- Medicaid Disproportionate Share Hospital (DSH) payment reductions were modified.

Background

On March 23, 2010, the President signed into law H.R. 3590, the Patient Protection and Affordable Care Act (PPACA; P.L. 111-148), as passed by the Senate on December 24, 2009, and the House on March 21, 2010. PPACA, among other changes, modified Medicaid and the Children's Health Insurance Program (CHIP) statutes. On March 21, 2010, the House passed an amendment in the nature of a substitute to H.R. 4872, the Health Care and Education Reconciliation Act of 2010 (HCERA, P.L. 111-152). After being passed by the House, HCERA was subsequently amended and passed by the Senate before being approved again by the House on March 25, 2010. HCERA was signed by the President on March 30, 2010. HCERA, which amends PPACA, combined with PPACA to form the health care reform law.

HCERA includes the following two titles: (1) Coverage, Medicare, Medicaid, and Revenues, and (2) Education and Health. Title I contains provisions related to health care and revenues, including modifications made to PPACA. Title II includes amendments to the Higher Education Act of 1965, which authorizes most of the federal programs involving postsecondary education, and other health amendments, which include other changes to PPACA.

The Congressional Budget Office (CBO) and the Joint Committee on Taxation (JTC) issued a revised cost estimate on March 20, 2010, for enacting both H.R. 3590 (now PPACA) and HCERA with a manager's amendment. CBO estimated that PPACA and HCERA together will reduce federal budgets deficits by $143 billion over the 2010-2019 period as a result of changes in direct spending and revenue. CBO's $143 billion estimate is composed of $124 billion in expenditure reductions and revenue from health care provisions and $19 billion in spending reductions from education.[1] CBO previously had issued a preliminary cost estimate for PPACA and HCERA. In CBO's preliminary estimate, PPACA and HCERA would have reduced federal deficits by $138 billion (for health care and education) over the 2010-2019 period.[2] CBO and JTC previously estimated that H.R. 3590 by itself would yield a net reduction in federal deficits of $118 billion over the 2010-2019 period.[3]

This report provides a brief summary of PPACA followed by a discussion of the modifications made by HCERA to the Medicaid and CHIP provisions in PPACA.

Summary of PPACA

PPACA consists of 10 titles that cover a variety of topics. In general, this law extends health insurance coverage to many currently uninsured Americans. It also has provisions to reduce expenditures, increase care coordination, encourage more use of health prevention, and improve quality of care. PPACA will reform the private health insurance market, impose a mandate for most legal U.S. residents to obtain health insurance, establish health insurance "Exchanges" that will subsidize health insurance coverage for eligible individuals; expand Medicaid eligibility; address healthcare workforce issues; and implement a number of other Medicaid and Medicare program and federal tax code changes. Key Medicaid and CHIP provisions in PPACA are summarized below.

- *Eligibility-related reforms.* PPACA will require states to expand Medicaid to certain individuals who are under age 65 with income up to 133% of the federal poverty level (FPL). This reform not only expands eligibility to a group who is not currently eligible for Medicaid (low income childless adults), but also raises Medicaid's mandatory income eligibility level for certain existing groups from 100% to 133% of the FPL.
- *Maintenance of effort provisions.* PPACA will require states to maintain current Medicaid and CHIP coverage levels—through 2013 for adults and 2019 for children.
- *Outreach and enrollment provisions.* PPACA includes provisions to encourage states to improve outreach, streamline enrollment, and coordinate with the proposed American Health Benefit Exchanges (Exchange).[4]
- *Benefit reforms.* PPACA will add new mandatory and optional benefits to Medicaid. Such mandatory benefits include premium assistance for employer- sponsored health insurance, coverage of free-standing birth clinics, and tobacco cessation services for pregnant woman. The law also authorizes states to offer new optional benefits such as preventive services for adults, health homes for persons with chronic conditions, and additional options for states to expand home- and community-based services as an alternative to institutional care.

- *Financing reforms*. PPACA introduces measures to reduce the growth of Medicaid expenditures and increases federal matching payments for the eligibility expansions.
- *Cost control reforms.* Some of the PPACA's cost control measures include (1) proposed reductions in Medicaid disproportionate share hospital (DSH) payments, (2) expenditure reductions for prescription drugs, and (3) payment reforms to reduce inappropriate hospital expenditures for health care-acquired conditions.
- *Program integrity reforms.* PPACA creates enforcement and monitoring tools and imposes new data reporting and oversight requirements on states and providers. States will also be required to implement initiatives used by the Medicare program, such as a national correct coding initiative and a recovery audit contract program for their Medicaid programs.
- *Nursing home accountability.* PPACA adds a number of requirements to improve the transparency of information within facilities and chains, as well as provides long-term care (LTC) consumers with information on the quality and performance of nursing homes.
- *Demonstrations, pilot programs, and grants.* PPACA will provide the Secretary of the Department of Health and Human Services (the Secretary) and state Medicaid and CHIP programs with opportunities to test models for improving the delivery, quality, and payment of services.
- *CHIP-related provisions.* PPACA requires states to maintain the current CHIP structure through FY2019, but does not provide federal CHIP appropriations beyond FY2013.
- *Miscellaneous Medicaid and CHIP reforms.* PPACA adds several offices within the Centers for Medicare and Medicaid Services (CMS) to better coordinate care across the Medicare and Medicaid/CHIP programs. One of these offices will be dedicated to improving coordination for beneficiaries eligible for both Medicare and Medicaid (dual eligibles). Another will add a Medicare and Medicaid Innovation Center to develop and test new payment and service delivery models to reduce Medicare, Medicaid, and CHIP expenditures, while preserving and enhancing quality of care for beneficiaries.

Medicaid and CHIP Modifications to PPACA by HCERA

The health care-related provisions in Title I of the HCERA modifies selected provisions in PPACA. What follows is a brief discussion of these Medicaid and CHIP-related changes. Each section contains a brief description of existing Medicaid law and related background, an explanation of the provision in PPACA, and a discussion of the changes enacted under HCERA.

Federal Funding for the States

To qualify for Medicaid, an individual must meet both categorical (i.e., must be a member of a covered group such as children, pregnant women, families with dependent children, the elderly, or the disabled) and financial eligibility requirements. Generally, Medicaid's financial requirements place limits on the maximum amount of income, and also sometimes, assets, that individuals may possess to participate. Additional guidelines specify how states should calculate these amounts. The specific income and asset limitations that apply to each eligibility group are set through a combination of federal parameters and state definitions. Consequently, these standards vary across states, and different standards apply to different population groups within states. Of the approximately 50 different eligibility "pathways" into Medicaid, some are mandatory while others may be covered at state option.

The federal government's share of Medicaid costs is determined by a formula in statute. This formula, referred to as the federal medical assistance percentage (FMAP), provides higher reimbursement to states with lower per capita income relative to the national average (and vice versa). FMAPs have a statutory minimum of 50% and a maximum of 83%, although some Medicaid services receive a higher federal match rate. In February 2009, with the passage of the American Recovery and Reinvestment Act of 2009 (ARRA, P.L. 111-5), states received temporary enhanced FMAP rates for nine fiscal quarters beginning with the first quarter of FY2009 and running through the first quarter of FY20 11 (December 31, 2010).

Subject to specified requirements, PPACA requires states to make eligible for Medicaid qualifying individuals with income up to 133% of the FPL beginning in 2014, among other mandatory expansions. Under this law, "newly eligible" individuals will be defined as non- elderly, non-pregnant individuals (e.g., childless adults, and certain parents), who are otherwise ineligible for Medicaid under prior law.[5] As a conforming measure, PPACA also will change the mandatory Medicaid income eligibility level for children age 6 to 19 from 100% FPL to 133% FPL (as previously applied to children under age 6). Income eligibility for individuals in the "newly eligible" population, other non-elderly individuals eligible under prior law (subject to certain exceptions), and certain CHIP eligible individuals will be based on modified gross income (MGI), or in the case of families, the household income. "Newly eligible" individuals will receive either benchmark or benchmark-equivalent coverage consistent with the requirements of Section 1937 of the Social Security Act (SSA)—excluding the "newly eligible" who meet the definition of exempted populations under this section, such as blind or disabled persons, and hospice patients, for example.

Under PPACA, states will receive 100% FMAP for the cost of care provided to "newly eligible" populations, from 2014 through 2016. Beginning in 2017, all states except Nebraska will have an FMAP lower than 100% for "newly eligibles" and will be grouped in the following two categories: (1) expansion states (those that, as of December 1, 2009, had statewide Medicaid coverage[6] for parents and childless adults up to 100% FPL); and (2) non-expansion states. Subject to a ceiling of 95%, for "newly eligible beneficiaries," expansion states will receive a 30.3 percentage point increase over their regular FMAP for 2017, a 31.3 percentage point increase over their regular FMAP for 2018, and a 32.3 percentage point increase for 2019, and thereafter. (See **Table 1** for a summary of these annual federal financial participation rates for new eligibles under PPACA and HCERA.)

Expansion states that do *not* get any additional FMAP (because no individuals qualified as "newly eligible" due to the states' prior Medicaid expansions), and that had not been granted a Secretary-approved diversion of DSH payments toward Medicaid coverage (effective in July 2009) will receive a 2.2 percentage point increase to their regular FMAP for existing Medicaid eligibility groups, between January 1, 2014, and September 30, 2019. Finally, under PPACA, between January 1, 2014, and December 31, 2016, a state can receive a 0.5 percentage point increase to its regular FMAP rate for existing Medicaid eligibility groups if the following two conditions are met: (1) it is a state that did *not* get any additional FMAP (because no individuals qualify as "newly eligible" due to the state's prior Medicaid expansions); and (2) it ranked as the state with the highest percentage of insured individuals in 2008 based on the Current Population Survey (CPS) (i.e., Massachusetts).

HCERA (Sec. 1201-1202) makes the following modifications to the financing portion of the eligibility provisions in PPACA:[7]

- FMAP rates for the cost of care provided to "newly eligible" populations for *all* states (i.e., expansion and non-expansion states) would be equal to 100% in 2014-2016, 95% in 2017, 94% in 2018, 93% in 2019, and 90% in 2020 and beyond (see **Table 1**).
- The provision in PPACA that provides the state of Nebraska with a permanent FMAP rate of 100% for "newly eligibles" was repealed.
- The length of time that specified expansion states would receive a 2.2 percentage point increase to their regular FMAP for existing Medicaid eligibility groups, was shortened from January 1, 2014, through September 30, 2019, to January 1, 2014, through December 31, 2015.
- The Massachusetts-specific 0.5 percentage point increase in FMAP for the period between January 1, 2014, and December 31, 2016 was repealed.
- Expansion states will receive an increase above their regular FMAP rate for the cost of care provided to currently eligible childless adults. The amount of the increase will be a certain percentage (i.e., a transition percentage)[8] of the difference between the state's regular FMAP and the FMAP it received for "newly eligibles" (see **Table 1**).

Income Definitions

Generally, Medicaid's financial requirements place limits on the maximum amount of income, and also sometimes, assets, that individuals may possess to participate. Additional guidelines specify how states should calculate these amounts. The specific income and asset limitations that apply to each eligibility group are set through a combination of federal parameters and state definitions. Consequently, these standards vary across states, and different standards apply to different population groups within states.

Under PPACA, certain income disregards (i.e., expenses such as child care costs or block of income disregards where a specified portion of family income is not counted), and assets or resource tests will no longer apply when assessing an individual's income to determine financial eligibility for Medicaid.

Table 1. FMAP Rates for Required Medicaid Expansions to Newly Eligible Populations under PPACA and HCERA; FYs 2013-2020

	2013	2014	2015	2016	2017	2018	2019	2020+
PPACA								
Expansion States	NA	100%	100%	100%	FMAP+30.3 (80.3%-95%)	FMAP+31.3 (81.3%-95%)	FMAP+32.3 (82.3%-95%)	FMAP+32.3 (82.3%-95%)
Non-expan-sion states	NA	100%	100%	100%	FMAP+34.3 (84.3%-95%)	FMAP+33.3 (83.3%-95%)	FMAP+32.3 (82.3%-95%)	FMAP+32.3 (82.3%-95%)
Nebraska	NA	100%	100%	100%	100%	100%	100%	100%
HCERA								
All states	NA	100%	100%	100%	95%	94%	93%	90%
Previously eligible childless adults in expansion states	NA	FMAP+ transition percentage (75%-95%)	FMAP+ transition percentage (80%-92%)	FMAP+ transition percentage (85%-94%)	FMAP+ transition percentage (86%-92%)	FMAP+ transition percentage (90%-92.6%)	FMAP+ transition percentage (93%)	FMAP+ transition percentage (90%)

Source: Table prepared by CRS Specialist in Health Care Financing, Chris L. Peterson, based on provisions in PPACA and HCERA.

Notes: "NA" means not applicable because the mandatory expansions will not take effect under PPACA or HCERA until 2014. FMAP under PPACA refers to the regular Medicaid matching percentage as typically calculated, with additional percentage points as shown, subject to a 95% cap on the FMAP (not shown). For example, in FY20 17 the FMAP rate for costs associated with "newly eligible" individuals in an expansion state with a regular FMAP rate of 54% will be increased by 30.3 percentage points for a new FMAP rate of 84.3%. The FMAP ranges (in parentheses) under PPACA and HCERA represent the potential FMAP rate based on regular FMAPs ranging from the statutory minimum (50%) to 80%. Although the Department of Health and Human Services will make the official determination of which states will be considered "expansion states" under PPACA and the HCERA, existing Medicaid eligibility information suggests that 11 states and the District of Columbia meet this definition including Arizona, Delaware, Hawaii, Maine, Massachusetts, Minnesota, New York, Pennsylvania, Vermont, Washington, and Wisconsin.

Instead, income eligibility for newly eligible individuals, non-elderly individuals eligible under prior law (subject to certain exceptions), as well as certain CHIP eligible individuals will be based on Modified Gross Income (MGI), or in the case of an individual in a family greater than one, the household income of such family.[9] MGI and household income will also be used to determine applicable premium and cost-sharing amounts under the state plan or waiver. MGI is defined as gross income decreased by trade and business deductions, losses from sale of property, and alimony payments, but including tax-exempt interest and income earned in the territories and by U.S. citizens or residents living abroad. Medicaid enrollees who otherwise would lose coverage because of the change in income-counting will be able to maintain eligibility.

Under HCERA (Sec. 1004), income eligibility for newly eligible individuals, non-elderly individuals eligible under prior law (subject to certain exceptions), as well as certain CHIP eligible individuals will be based on modified adjusted gross income (MAGI),[10] or in the case of an individual in a family greater than one, the household income of such family. MAGI and household income will also be used to determine applicable premium and cost-sharing amounts under the state plan or waiver.

MAGI is defined as the Internal Revenue Code's (IRC's) *Adjusted Gross Income* (AGI), which reflects a number of deductions, including trade and business deductions, losses from sale of property, and alimony payments, increased by tax-exempt interest and income earned by U.S. citizens or residents living abroad. Although PPACA prohibits any continued use of income disregards under Medicaid once the new income definitions are in place, the reconciliation bill (Sec. 1004(e)) will require states determining individuals' Medicaid eligibility under MAGI to reduce their countable income by a certain amount. That amount will be 5% of the upper income limit for that Medicaid eligibility pathway.

Payments to Primary Care Providers

State Medicaid plans must provide methods and procedures to assure that payments are consistent with efficiency, economy, and quality of care, and are sufficient to enlist enough providers so that care and services are available at least to the extent that such care is available to the general population in the geographic area. Additional requirements regarding payment rates under Medicaid apply to inpatient hospital and long-term care facility services.

However, within these guidelines, states have considerable flexibility to set provider reimbursement rates independent of any national baseline or reference.

PPACA did not have a provision addressing payments to primary care providers. However, there was a provision in the Affordable Health Care for America Act (H.R. 3962), the health reform bill passed by the House. HCERA (Sec. 1202) will add similar language to PPACA. States will be required to set Medicaid payments for primary care services (i.e., evaluation and management or E&M services defined by Medicare as of December 31, 2009, and as subsequently modified by the Secretary, and services related to immunization administration for vaccines and toxoids) relative to Medicare payment rates. Primary care services furnished in 2013 and 2014 by a physician with a primary specialty designation of family medicine, general internal medicine, or pediatric medicine will be paid at the Medicare rate for these services or higher (or if greater, the Medicare 2009 payment rate that will be applicable).

With respect to Medicaid managed care, the bill also will require that, in the case of E&M services, these new payment rates will apply, regardless of the manner in which such payments are made, including in the form of capitation or partial capitation (e.g., payments made on a "per member per month" basis, rather than for each specific unit of service delivered).

For services furnished in 2013 and 2014, the federal government will fully finance the portion of primary care service payments by which the new minimum payment rates exceed the state's existing payment rates as of July 1, 2009. That is the federal FMAP percentage for the additional costs born by a state will equal 100%.

Disproportionate Share Hospital Payments

Under Medicaid, states are required to make disproportionate share hospital (DSH) adjustments to the payment rates of hospitals treating large numbers of low-income and Medicaid patients. The DSH provision is intended to recognize the disadvantaged situation of those hospitals. In claiming federal matching dollars, states cannot exceed their state-specific allotment amounts, calculated for each state based on a statutory formula. States must define, in their state Medicaid plans, hospitals that qualify as DSH hospitals and their DSH payment formulas. DSH hospitals must include at least all hospitals meeting minimum criteria and may not include hospitals that have a Medicaid utilization rate below 1%. The DSH payment formula also must meet minimum criteria, and DSH payments for any specific hospital cannot exceed a hospital-specific cap based on the unreimbursed costs of providing hospital services to Medicaid and uninsured patients.

In determining federal DSH allotments for states, special rules apply to "low DSH states" (those in which total DSH payments for FY2000 were less than 3% of the state's total Medicaid spending on benefits). For low DSH states for FY2004 through FY2008, the allotment for each of these years was equal to 16% more than the prior year's amount. For years beginning in FY2009, DSH allotments for all states are equal to the prior year amount increased by the change in the consumer price index for all urban consumers (CPI-U). For FY2009, federal DSH allotments across states and the District of Columbia totaled to nearly $10.6 billion. Provisions under ARRA provided additional temporary DSH funding for states that increases total federal DSH allotments to nearly $10.9 billion.

PPACA reduces federal DSH allotments to states based on changes (reductions) in state-specific uninsurance rates over time. State DSH allotments will remain intact as under current law until a state uninsurance level is reached. This level will be initially reached the first fiscal year after FY2012 for which a state's uninsured rate, as measured by the Census Bureau's American Community Survey, decreases by at least 45%, compared to an initial baseline uninsured rate for FY2009. Once this level is reached, reductions in DSH allotments will depend on a state's status as a low DSH state and spending patterns in comparison to a benchmark (over or under 99.90% of the state's average DSH allotments) during a base five-year period (FY2004 through FY2008).

These reductions will be 17.5% (over the spending benchmark) or 25% (under the spending benchmark) for low DSH states versus 35% (over the spending benchmark) or 50% (under the spending benchmark) for all other states. For subsequent years, if a state's uninsurance rate decreases further, the state's DSH allotment will be further reduced, again depending on a state's status as a low DSH state and its spending patterns during the base five-year period. In general, these reductions will be equal to the product of the percentage reduction in uncovered individuals and 20% (over the spending benchmark) or 27.5% (under the spending benchmark) for low DSH states versus 40% (over the spending benchmark) or 55% (under the spending benchmark) for all other states.

For FY2013 forward, in no case will a state's DSH allotment be less than 50% of the state's FY2012 allotment, increased by the percentage change in the CPI-U for each previous year occurring before the fiscal year. **Table 2** summarizes the DSH provisions in PPACA.

Under HCERA, the provision (Sec. 1203) strikes the language in PPACA and requires the Secretary to make aggregate reductions in Medicaid DSH allotments that would equal $500 million in FY2014, $600 million in FY2015, $600 million in FY2016, $1.8 billion in FY2017, $5.0 billion in FY2018, $5.6 billion in FY2019, and $4.0 billion in FY2020.

Table 2. DSH Provisions in P.L. 111-148

Trigger Year of DSH Allotment Changes	**DSH Allotment Reductions by Type of State (Based on Spending Patterns)**	
When a state's rate of uninsurance decreases by at least 45% compared to its 2009 rate, then:	States with annual DSH spending of >99.90% of average DSH spending for FY2004-FY2008	States with annual DSH spending <=99.90% of average DSH spending for FY2004-FY2008
First Fiscal Year After FY2012		
Low DSH States	(DSH Allotment)*(17.5%)	(DSH Allotment)*(25%)
All Other States	(DSH Allotment)*(35%)	(DSH Allotment)*(50%)
Subsequent Years		
Low DSH States	(Reduced DSH Allotment) * (% Annual Reduction in Uninsured)*(20%)	(Reduced DSH Allotment) * (% Annual Reduction in Uninsured)*(27.5%)
All Other States	(Reduced DSH Allotment)* (% Annual Reduction in Uninsured)*(40%)	(Reduced DSH Allotment) * (% Annual Reduction in Uninsured)*(55%)

Notes: For FY2013 forward, in no case would a state's DSH allocation be less than 50% of the state's FY2012 DSH allotment (increased by the CPI-U for each previous fiscal year). "*" means "multiplied by."

To achieve these aggregate reductions, the Secretary will be required to:

(1) impose the largest percentage reduction on states that

- have the lowest percentage of uninsured individuals (determined on the basis of data from the Bureau of the Census, audited hospital cost reports, and other information likely to yield accurate data) during the most recent fiscal year with available data, or

- do not target their DSH payments to hospitals with high volumes of Medicaid patients, and hospitals that have high levels of uncompensated care (excluding bad debt);

(2) impose a smaller percentage reduction on low DSH states; and
(3) take into account the extent to which the DSH allotment for a State was included in the budget neutrality calculation for a coverage expansion approved under Section 1115 as of July 31, 2009.

For each fiscal year, these reductions in DSH allotments will be applied on a quarterly basis. For a state with a DSH allotment of $0 in the second, third and fourth quarters of FY2012, the provision will set that state's DSH allotments at $47.2 million, and for a state with a DSH allotment of $0 in FY2013, the provision will set that state's DSH allotment at $53.1 million.

Funding for the Territories

The federal share for most Medicaid service costs is determined by the FMAP, which is based on a formula that provides higher reimbursement to states with lower per capita income relative to the national average (and vice versa). FMAPs have a statutory minimum of 50% and maximum of 83%. In the territories, the FMAP is typically set at 50%.

Medicaid programs in the five territories (American Samoa, Guam, the Northern Mariana Islands, Puerto Rico, and the Virgin Islands) are subject to annual federal spending caps that are set in statute. The Congress has increased the levels of federal Medicaid funding in the territories in recent years. For FY2008 and subsequent fiscal years, the total annual cap on federal funding for the Medicaid programs in the territories is calculated by increasing the FY2007 ceiling for inflation. The territories also benefited from a temporary 30% increase in their Medicaid spending caps as a result of the FMAP assistance provided under ARRA.

The territories also have access to other sources of federal matching funds; for example, they may be eligible for enhanced federal match (90% or 75%) that is available under Medicaid for improvements in data reporting systems. Beginning with FY2009, funds spent on specified administrative activities will not count against the Medicaid caps.

PPACA increases the spending caps for the territories by 30% for the second, third, and fourth quarters of FY2011, and for each full fiscal year thereafter. The law also increases the applicable FMAP by five percentage points—to 55%—beginning January 1, 2011, and for each full fiscal year thereafter. Beginning in fiscal year 2014, payments made to the territories for medical assistance for "newly eligible" individuals will not count towards territories' applicable Medicaid spending caps. In the case of the territories, the provision defines "newly eligible" individuals as non-pregnant childless adults who are eligible under the new Medicaid mandatory eligibility group and whose modified gross income or household income does not exceed the income eligibility level in effect for parents under each such commonwealth or territory's state plan or waiver as of the date of enactment of the bill.

HCERA (Sec. 1204) strikes the Medicaid provisions related to payment of the territories in PPACA, and permits territories to establish an Exchange (in accordance with the Exchange- related provisions also included in PPACA), not later than October 13, 2013. Out of funds not otherwise appropriated, $1.0 billion is appropriated for the period between 2014 and 2019 for the purpose of providing premium and cost-sharing assistance to residents of the territory to obtain health insurance coverage through the Exchange. Of this amount, the Secretary is to allocate $925 million for Puerto Rico, and a portion (as specified by the Secretary) of the remaining $75 million for any other territory that chooses establish an Exchange. Under this provision, territories are to be treated as states and required to structure their Exchanges in a manner so there is no gap in assistance between individuals eligible for Medicaid and those eligible for premium and cost- sharing assistance.

Also under HCERA, territories that do *not* elect to establish an Exchange as of the specified date are entitled to an increase in their existing Medicaid funding caps. For the period between July 1, 2011, and September 30, 2019, $6.3 billion dollars in total additional payments are available for distribution among each territory across each such year in an amount that is proportional to the capped amounts available to the territories under current law. Current law rules regarding funds spent on specified administrative activities will apply, and the provision is effective July 1, 2011.

Delay in Community First Choice Option

A personal care attendant provides assistance with activities of daily living (ADLs) and instrumental activities of daily living (IADLs) to persons with a significant disability. ADLs and IADLs include activities such as eating, bathing and showering, using the toilet, preparing meals, managing money, and shopping for groceries, among others. States have the option to cover personal care services, including personal care attendant services, under a variety of optional state plan benefits.

Under PPACA, states can offer home and community-based attendant services as an optional state plan benefit to Medicaid beneficiaries whose income does not exceed 150% of poverty, or if greater, the income level applicable for an individual who has been determined to require the level-of-care offered in an institution. This provision would be effective beginning October 1, 2010. However, under HCERA (Sec. 1205), this provision becomes effective on October 1, 2011.

Financing: Payment for Prescription Drugs

Outpatient prescription drugs are an optional Medicaid benefit, but all states cover prescription drugs for most beneficiary groups. Medicaid law requires prescription drug manufacturers who wish to sell their products to Medicaid agencies to agree to pay rebates to states for outpatient drugs purchased on behalf of Medicaid beneficiaries. Medicaid differentiates between the following two types of drugs when determining rebates:

1. single source innovator drugs (generally, those still under patent) and innovator multiple source drugs (originally marketed under a patent or an original new drug application, but for which there now are therapeutically or pharmaceutically equivalent products); and
2. all other, non-innovator, multiple source drugs.

Rebates for drugs still under patent or those once covered by patents have two components: a basic rebate and an additional rebate. Medicaid's basic rebate is determined by the larger of a drug's quarterly Average Manufacturer Price (AMP) compared to the best price for the same period, or a percentage (15.1%) of the drug's quarterly AMP. Drug manufacturers owe an additional rebate on single source innovator drugs (the first drug category mentioned above) when their unit prices for individual products increase faster than inflation.

PPACA requires manufacturers to pay additional rebates to Medicaid for certain new formulations of existing single source or innovator multiple source drugs. For these new drug formulations, referred to as line extensions, drug manufacturers will pay the additional rebate based on a new formula. Similar to the House health reform bill, H.R. 3962, HCERA (Sec. 1206) will limit the definition of line extension drugs to oral solid dosage forms of single source or innovator multiple source drugs.

PPACA also modifies the definition of Average Manufacturer Price (AMP). Among other changes to AMP, this law specifically excludes a wide range of rebates, discounts, price concessions, and service fees extended by manufacturers to wholesalers, retail community pharmacies, and other large volume purchasers. Under the reconciliation bill, the definition of AMP will be further modified to exclude discounts paid by manufacturers to Medicare Part D plans. The effect of excluding the Medicare Part D discounts, as well as other price concessions will be make the calculation of AMP more closely reflect the actual real average cost of outpatient prescription drugs. HCERA did not amend the Medicaid prescription drug provisions.

Program Integrity

Program integrity (PI) initiatives are designed to combat waste, fraud, and abuse. This includes processes directed at reducing improper payments, as well as activities to prevent, detect, investigate, and ultimately prosecute health care fraud and abuse. More specifically, PI ensures that correct payments are made to legitimate providers for appropriate and reasonable services for eligible beneficiaries.

Congress provided additional dedicated funding for Medicaid program integrity activities in the Deficit Reduction Act of 2005 (DRA, P.L. 109-171). Under DRA, among many other changes, Congress established a Medicaid Integrity Program (MIP) that included annual appropriations reaching $75 million. This MIP funding was to support and enhance state PI efforts by expanding and sustaining national PI activities in the areas of provider audits, overpayment identification, and payment integrity and quality of care education.

PPACA increased funding to the Health Care Fraud and Abuse Control (HCFAC) account. HCFAC funds are used for a number of health care fraud and abuse activities, but the majority of the funding goes to Medicare activities. HCERA (Sec. 1304) further increases those HCFAC account funds, bringing them up to the levels proposed in the House health care reform bill (H.R. 3962). In addition, HCERA increases Medicaid Program Integrity funds by indexing MIP funds to annual changes in the consumer price index, beginning with fiscal year 2010.

End Notes

[1] Congressional Budget Office, letter to Honorable Nancy Pelosi, March 20, 2010, available at http://www.cbo.gov/ ftpdocs/1 13xx/doc1 1379/Manager'sAmendmentto Reconciliation Proposal.pdf.

[2] Congressional Budget Office, letter to the Honorable Nancy Pelosi, March 18, 2010, available at http://www.cbo.gov/ ftpdocs/1 13xx/doc1 1355/hr4872.pdf.

[3] Congressional Budget Office, letter to the Honorable Harry Reid, March 11, 2010, available at http://www.cbo.gov/ ftpdocs/1 13xx/doc1 1307/Reid_Letter_HR3590.pdf.

[4] For a description of the Exchange, see CRS Report R40942, *Private Health Insurance Provisions in Senate-Passed H.R. 3590, the Patient Protection and Affordable Care Act* , by Hinda Chaikind et al.

[5] Like the House health reform bill (H.R. 3962), PPACA will not extend Medicaid eligibility to those also eligible for or enrolled in the Medicare program.

[6] To be considered an "expansion state," this Medicaid coverage must include inpatient hospital services and can not be limited to only the following benefits: premium assistance (or Medicaid coverage otherwise dependent on employer coverage or contribution), hospital-only plans, high-deductible health plans or Health Opportunity Accounts.

[7] Federal financial participation for some of the benefit-related provisions under PPACA (e.g., Adult Preventive Care) are tied to the FMAP rates states would receive for "newly eligible" populations. Federal financial participation for these provisions would also be impacted by the proposed changes to the FMAP rates for "Newly Eligible" populations under the reconciliation bill.

[8] The reconciliation bill defines the transition percentage as 50% in 2014, 60% in 2015, 70% in 2016, 80% in 2017, 90% in 2018, and 100% thereafter.

[9] MGI and household income would also be used for determining the amount of premium credit assistance for the purchase of a qualified health benefits plan under state exchanges, described in Section 1401 of the Senate bill. For more information on MGI and household income see CRS Report R40942, *Private Health Insurance Provisions in Senate-Passed H.R. 3590, the Patient Protection and Affordable Care Act* , by Hinda Chaikind et al.

[10] MAGI and household income would also be used for determining the amount of premium credit assistance for the purchase of a qualified health benefits plan under state exchanges, as described in Section 1401 of the Senate bill. For more information on MAGI and household income, see CRS Report R40942, *Private Health Insurance Provisions in Senate-Passed H.R. 3590, the Patient Protection and Affordable Care Act* , by Hinda Chaikind et al.

In: Medicaid, Children's Health Insurance… ISBN: 978-1-61122-903-5
Editors: A. T. Dupont and S. L. Peeters © 2011 Nova Science Publishers, Inc.

Chapter 2

Medicaid and the State Children's Health Insurance Program (CHIP) Provisions in PPACA: Summary and Timeline*

Julie Stone, Evelyne P. Baumrucker, Cliff Binder, Elicia J. Herz, Elayne J. Heisler and Alexandra J. Rothenburger

Summary

The President signed into law H.R. 3590, the Patient Protection and Affordable Care Act (PPACA; P.L. 111-148), on March 23, 2010. Seven days later, a second bill, H.R. 4872, was signed into law by the President to modify PPACA. This second law, the Health Care and Education Reconciliation Act of 2010 (HCERA; P.L. 111-152), was signed into law on March 30, 2010. Together these measures constitute what is referred to as the health care reform law, which makes many significant changes to the private and public markets for health insurance, as well as modifies aspects of the publicly financed health care delivery system. It represents the most significant reform

* This is an edited, reformatted and augmented edition of a United States Congressional Research Service publication, Report R41210, dated August 19, 2010.

to the Medicaid program since its establishment in 1965. This report details some of the major changes to the Medicaid and CHIP programs and provides a timeline of effective dates for these provisions.

In general, the Medicaid law (1) raises Medicaid income eligibility levels for certain people up to 133% of the federal poverty level, (2) adds both mandatory and optional benefits to Medicaid, (3) increases the federal matching payments for certain groups of beneficiaries and for particular services provided, (4) provides new requirements and incentives for states to improve quality of care and encourage more use of preventive services, and (5) makes a number of other Medicaid program changes. Regarding CHIP, the law includes a new requirement for states to maintain their current program structures through FY2019 and extends additional CHIP funding through FY2015.

To help explain the most important Medicaid and CHIP changes, provision descriptions are grouped into the following six major issue areas: eligibility, benefits, financing, program integrity, demonstrations and grant funding, and miscellaneous. **Appendix A** provides a detailed implementation timeline of the Medicaid and CHIP provisions. **Appendix B** is a crosswalk between the provision titles and the amending sections of P.L. 111-148 and P.L. 111-152 for all of the Medicaid and CHIP provisions. Finally, **Appendix C** is a list of abbreviations used in this report and their definitions. This report will be updated as needed

Introduction

The President signed into law H.R. 3590, the Patient Protection and Affordable Care Act (PPACA; P.L. 111-148), on March 23, 2010. Seven days later, a second bill, H.R. 4872, was signed into law by the President to modify PPACA. This second law, the Health Care and Education Reconciliation Act of 2010 (the Reconciliation Act or HCERA; P.L. 111-152), was signed into law on March 30, 2010. Together these measures constitute what is referred to as the health care reform law, which makes many significant changes to the private and public markets for health insurance, as well as modifies aspects of the publicly financed health care delivery system. It represents the most significant reform to the Medicaid program since its establishment in 1965. This report highlights some of the major changes to the Medicaid and CHIP programs and provides a timeline of effective dates for these provisions.

In general, the Medicaid law (1) raises Medicaid income eligibility levels for certain people up to 133% of the federal poverty level, (2) adds both mandatory and optional benefits to Medicaid, (3) increases the federal matching payments for certain groups of beneficiaries and for particular services provided, (4) provides new requirements and incentives for states to improve quality of care and encourage more use of preventive services, and (5) makes a number of other Medicaid program changes. Regarding CHIP, the law includes a new requirement for states to maintain their current program structures through FY2019 and extends additional CHIP funding through FY2015.

To help explain the most important Medicaid and CHIP changes, provision descriptions are grouped into the following six major issue areas: eligibility, benefits, financing, program integrity, demonstrations and grant funding, and miscellaneous. **Appendix A** provides a detailed implementation timeline of the Medicaid and CHIP provisions. Appendix B is a crosswalk between the provision titles and the amending sections of P.L. 111-148 and P.L. 111-152 for all of the Medicaid and CHIP provisions. Finally, **Appendix C** is a list of abbreviations used in this report and their definitions.

Congressional Budget Office and Joint Committee on Taxation Analysis

The Congressional Budget Office (CBO) and the Joint Committee on Taxation (JCT) issued a cost estimate on March 20, 2010, for PPACA and HCERA. CBO estimated that PPACA and the HCERA will reduce federal budget deficits by $143 billion over the FY2010-FY2019 period as a result of changes in direct spending and revenue. CBO's $143 billion estimate is composed of $124 billion in reductions and revenue from health care provisions and $19 billion in spending reductions from education.[1] CBO and JCT previously estimated that PPACA by itself would reduce federal deficits by $118 billion over the 2010-2019 period.[2]

Overview of the Medicaid and CHIP Provisions in the Health Reform Law

Key Medicaid and CHIP provisions included in the health reform law are summarized below.

- *Eligibility-related reforms.* Beginning in 2014, or sooner at state option, the law requires states to expand Medicaid to certain individuals who are under age 65 with income up to 133% of the federal poverty level (FPL). This reform not only expands eligibility to a group that is not currently eligible for Medicaid (low income childless adults), but also raises Medicaid's mandatory income eligibility level for certain existing groups to 133% of the FPL. This represents the single largest eligibility expansion since the start of the program in 1965. The law also modifies income counting rules when determining Medicaid eligibility for certain populations.[3] From 2014 to 2016, the federal government will cover 100% of the Medicaid costs of these "newly eligible" individuals, with the percentage dropping to 90% by 2020. States cover the percentage not paid by the federal government.
- *Maintenance of effort provisions.* The law requires states to maintain current Medicaid and CHIP eligibility levels through 2013 (or when the Secretary determines that the state exchange is fully operational) for adults and 2019 for children.
- *Outreach and enrollment provisions.* The law includes provisions to encourage states to improve outreach, streamline enrollment, and coordinate with the proposed American Health Benefit Exchanges (exchanges).[4]
- *Benefit reforms.* The law adds new mandatory and optional benefits to Medicaid. Such mandatory benefits include coverage of free-standing birth clinics, and tobacco cessation services for pregnant woman. The law also authorizes states to offer new optional benefits such as preventive services for adults and health homes for persons with chronic conditions. Additional options for states to expand home and community-based services as an alternative to institutional care are also included.
- *Payment and financing reforms.* Some of the law's reforms affecting payments and financing include (1) increases in federal matching

payments for the "newly eligible" individuals in the eligibility expansions up to 133% FPL, (2) reductions in Medicaid disproportionate share hospital (DSH) allotments, (3) expenditure reductions for prescription drugs including revising the definition of the average manufacture's price (AMP) to help make AMP more closely reflect prices retail community pharmacies pay for prescription drugs, (4) reductions in inappropriate hospital expenditures for health care-acquired conditions, and (5) increases in primary care physician payment rates for selected services.

- *Increased funding for the territories.* The law permits the territories to establish exchanges and provides federal funds for premium and cost-sharing assistance for individuals who obtain health insurance coverage through an exchange. Territories that do not opt to establish an exchange will receive an increase in their Medicaid spending caps. The law also increases the Medicaid FMAP rate available to all of the territories from 50% to 55% beginning with the fourth quarter of FY2011.
- *Program integrity reforms.* The law creates enforcement and monitoring tools and imposes new data reporting and oversight requirements on states and providers. States will also be required to implement initiatives used by the Medicare program, such as a national correct coding initiative and a recovery audit contract program for their Medicaid programs. The law provides additional program integrity funding through indexing of the Medicaid Integrity Program for fiscal years beginning with FY2010.
- *Nursing home accountability.* The law adds a number of requirements to improve the transparency of information within facilities and chains, and provides longterm care (LTC) consumers with information on the quality and performance of nursing homes.
- *Demonstrations, pilot programs, and grants.* The law provides the Secretary of the Department of Health and Human Services (the Secretary) and state Medicaid and CHIP programs with opportunities to test models for improving the delivery, quality, and cost of services.
- *CHIP-related provisions.* The law requires states to maintain the current CHIP structure through FY2019, but does not provide federal CHIP appropriations beyond FY2015, at which point, if future appropriations are insufficient, CHIP children will obtain comparable coverage through the exchanges or Medicaid, as applicable. If new

funding is made available, states will receive higher federal matching rates for CHIP services beginning in FY2016. Upon enactment, states are required to maintain CHIP eligibility levels through FY2019 as a condition of receiving federal matching funds for Medicaid expenditures (notwithstanding the lack of corresponding federal CHIP appropriations for FY2016 through FY2019).

- *Miscellaneous Medicaid and CHIP reforms*. The law adds several offices within the Centers for Medicare and Medicaid Services (CMS) to better coordinate care across the Medicare and Medicaid/CHIP programs. One of these offices will be dedicated to improving coordination for beneficiaries eligible for both Medicare and Medicaid (dual eligibles). Another will add a Medicare and Medicaid Innovation Center to develop and test new payment and service delivery models to reduce Medicare, Medicaid, and CHIP expenditures, while preserving and enhancing quality of care for beneficiaries.

Eligibility

Medicaid is a means-tested entitlement program operated by states within broad federal guidelines. To qualify, an individual must meet both categorical (i.e., must be a member of a covered group, such as children, pregnant women, families with dependent children, the elderly, or the disabled) and financial eligibility requirements.

Of the approximately 50 different eligibility "pathways" into Medicaid, including those that existed even before the health reform law was enacted, some are mandatory while others may be offered at state option. Examples of groups that states must provide Medicaid to include pregnant women and children below specified income levels and poor individuals with disabilities or poor individuals over age 64 who qualify for cash assistance under the Supplemental Security Income (S SI) program. Examples of groups that states may choose to cover under Medicaid include pregnant women and infants with family income between 133% FPL and 185% FPL, and "medically needy" individuals who meet categorical requirements with income up to 133% of the maximum payment amount applicable under states' former Aid to Families with Dependent Children (AFDC) programs based on family size.[5] Under prior law, "childless adults" (nonelderly adults who are not disabled, not pregnant and not parents of dependent children) were generally *not* eligible for Medicaid, regardless of their income.

The health reform law makes several changes to Medicaid eligibility. PPACA adds two new mandatory eligibility groups, and several new optional eligibility groups. In addition, it makes several modifications to existing eligibility groups, changes the way income is counted for certain groups to determine if an individual meets Medicaid's income eligibility requirements, and adds provisions to facilitate outreach and enrollment in Medicaid, CHIP, and the Health Insurance exchanges.[6] In their March 20, 2010, final cost estimate for PPACA and HCERA, CBO and JCT estimated that coverage expansion provisions in the health reform law would result in a Medicaid enrollment increase over the baseline of approximately 16 million by FY2019.[7]

Medicaid and Health Insurance Reform

Medicaid Coverage for the Lowest-Income Populations

(P.L. 111-148: §2001 as modified by §10201; P.L. 111-152: §1004 and §1201)

Beginning in 2014, the health reform law creates a new mandatory Medicaid eligibility group for all nonelderly, nonpregnant individuals (e.g., childless adults, certain parents, certain people with disabilities) who are not entitled to or enrolled in Medicare Part A or enrolled in Medicare Part B, and are otherwise ineligible for Medicaid. For such individuals, the provision establishes 133% of FPL based on modified adjusted gross income (or MAGI as described below) as the new mandatory minimum Medicaid income eligibility level.[8] The law also specifies that an income disregard in the amount of 5% FPL will be deducted from an individual's income when determining Medicaid eligibility based on MAGI, thus the effective upper income eligibility threshold for such individuals in this new eligibility group will be 138% FPL.[9] Additional federal financial assistance will be paid to all states to share in the cost of care provided to those in the new eligibility group who meet the definition of "newly eligible." (These financing arrangements are described in more detail under the financing section of this report.)

As a conforming measure, the provision also changes the mandatory Medicaid income eligibility level for poverty-related children ages 6 to 19 from 100% FPL to 133% FPL (as applied under prior law to children under age 6). MAGI income counting rules and the 5% income disregard will apply to all poverty-related children (except those determined eligible through an Express Lane eligibility determination as permitted under the State Children's Health Insurance Reauthorization Act, CHIPRA, P.L. 111-3). Thus, in 2014, most nonelderly citizens up to 138% FPL (i.e., 133% FPL with the 5% FPL income disregard) will be eligible for Medicaid.

During the transitional period between April 1, 2010, and January 1, 2014, states will have the option to expand Medicaid to individuals eligible under the new eligibility group up to 133% FPL as long as the state does not extend coverage to (1) individuals with higher income before those with lower income or (2) parents unless their children are enrolled in the state plan, a waiver, or in other health coverage. Prior to 2014, states are not required to use the MAGI income counting rules when determining income eligibility for the new eligibility group up to 133% FPL. States that pick up this option may apply a different income counting methodology (e.g., SSI's income counting rules) as long as it is approved by the Secretary.[10] Finally, during the optional phase-in period no additional federal financial assistance will be available for the cost of care associated with these individuals.

The provision also allows states to make a "presumptive eligibility" determination for individuals eligible for the new eligibility group or for individuals eligible for family coverage under Section 1931 of the Social Security Act (SSA),[11] if the state already allows for presumptive eligibility determinations for children or pregnant women subject to guidance established by the Secretary. That is, states may enroll such individuals for a limited period of time, before completed Medicaid applications are filed and processed, based on a preliminary determination by Medicaid providers of likely Medicaid eligibility. Such individuals must then formally apply for coverage within a certain timeframe to continue receiving Medicaid benefits. Under prior law, presumptive eligibility determinations could only be made for children, pregnant women, certain women with breast or cervical cancer.

Financial Eligibility Requirements for Individuals Eligible under the New Eligibility Group up to 133% FPL and Other Nonelderly Populations Determined Using Modified Adjusted Gross Income (MAGI)

(P.L. 111-148: §2001 as modified by §10201; P.L. 111-152: §1004)

Generally, Medicaid's financial eligibility requirements place limits on the maximum amount of income (and sometimes assets) that individuals may possess to participate. Additional guidelines specify how states should calculate these amounts. The specific income and asset limitations that apply to each eligibility group are set through a combination of federal parameters and state definitions. Consequently, these standards vary across states, and different standards apply to different population groups within states.

Under PPACA, asset tests and certain income disregards (e.g., type of expenses such as child care costs or block of income disregards where a specified portion of family income is not counted) will no longer be used to assess the financial eligibility of (1) individuals eligible under the new eligibility group up to 133% FPL, (2) other nonelderly populations eligible under prior law (subject to certain exceptions as specified below in the subsection titled "Financial Eligibility Requirements for Certain Populations Eligible Under Prior Law"), and (3) certain Medicaid or CHIP-eligible children. The new income test for these individuals will be based on MAGI.[12]

MAGI is defined as the Internal Revenue Code's (IRC's) *adjusted gross income (AGI)* plus certain foreign earned income and tax-exempt interest. AGI reflects a number of deductions, including trade and business deductions, losses from sale of property, and alimony payments, increased by tax-exempt interest and income earned by U.S. citizens or residents living abroad. Although PPACA prohibits any continued use of income disregards under Medicaid once the new income definitions are in place, HCERA (Section 1004(e)) requires states determining individuals' Medicaid eligibility under MAGI to reduce their countable income by a certain amount. That amount will be 5% of the upper income limit for that Medicaid eligibility pathway. MAGI will also be used to determine applicable premium and cost sharing amounts under the state plan or waiver. In addition to these income counting changes, for populations whose eligibility is determined using MAGI, states are prohibited from applying any assets or resources test.

Financial Eligibility Requirements for Certain Populations Eligible under Prior Law

(P.L. 111-148: §2001 and §2002 as modified by §10201)

Under the health reform law, certain groups are exempted from income eligibility determinations based on MAGI. Prior law's income counting rules under Medicaid will continue to be used for determining eligibility for certain groups, including (1) individuals who are eligible for Medicaid through another federal or state assistance program (e.g., foster care children and individuals receiving SSI), (2) the elderly, (3) certain disabled individuals who qualify for Medicaid on the basis of being blind or disabled without regard to whether the individual is eligible for SSI, (4) the medically needy, and (5) enrollees in a Medicare Savings Program (e.g., Qualified Medicare Beneficiaries for which Medicaid pays the Medicare premiums, and/or coinsurance and deductibles). In addition, MAGI does not affect eligibility determinations through Express Lane (to determine whether a child has met Medicaid or CHIP eligibility requirements), for Medicare prescription drug low-income subsidies, or for determinations of eligibility for Medicaid long term care services.[13]

Any individual enrolled in Medicaid (under the state plan or a waiver) on January 1, 2014, who is determined ineligible for medical assistance solely because of the application of the new MAGI income counting rule will remain Medicaid eligible (and subject to the same premiums and cost- sharing as applied to the individual on that date) until the later of March 31, 2014, or his/her next Medicaid eligibility redetermination date. At that point such persons could purchase insurance, with the help of subsidies, through state exchanges. With regard to children, the law requires that the transition to MAGI cannot result in the loss Medicaid eligibility for individuals who would have been eligible for Medicaid as of March 23, 2010.

Finally, state use of MAGI to determine income eligibility for Medicaid (and for any other purposes applicable under the state plan) will not affect or limit the application of (1) the state plan requirement to determine an individual's income at the point in time at which a Medicaid application is processed or (2) Medicaid rules regarding sources of countable income.

In general, these provisions take effect on January 1, 2014. For a state that chooses to transition to MAGI earlier, these provisions take effect upon the enactment of an individual state's law.

Medicaid Benefit Coverage for The New Mandatory Eligibility Group

(P.L. 111-148: §2001 as modified by §10201)

Medicaid's standard benefits are identified in federal statute and regulations and include a wide range of medical services. Some Medicaid benefits are mandatory, meaning they must be made available by states to the majority of Medicaid populations (i.e., those classified as "categorically needy"), while other benefits may be covered at state option. As an alternative to providing all of the mandatory and selected optional benefits under traditional Medicaid, states have the option to enroll certain state-specified groups in benchmark and benchmark-equivalent benefit plans, as permitted under Section 1937 of the SSA. (For more information on benchmark and benchmark- equivalent coverage, including the recently enacted changes to this coverage, see the "Benefits" section of this report.)

Enrollees in the new eligibility group up to 133% FPL will receive either benchmark or benchmark-equivalent coverage consistent with the requirements of Section 1937 of the SSA.[14]

Section 1937 excludes certain groups from mandatory enrollment in benchmark or benchmark- equivalent coverage, including individuals with special medical needs and medically frail individuals.

Specifically, some individuals with disabilities who are not currently eligible for a state's Medicaid program—either because they meet the Supplemental Security Income (SSI) program's definition of disability (used to determine disability for a number of Medicaid's eligibility groups) but have income that exceeds their state's income threshold or have a disability that does not qualify under the SSI definition—may qualify for Medicaid under the new eligibility group. These individuals would likely be exempt from mandatory enrollment in benchmark and benchmark-equivalent coverage and as a result may be entitled to the state's more comprehensive package of state plan services, including long-term care benefits for certain enrollees.

Finally (as per the requirements of Section 1937), children receiving benchmark and benchmark- equivalent coverage must receive all Early and Periodic Screening, Diagnostic, and Treatment (EPSDT) services.

Maintenance of Medicaid Income Eligibility (MOE)

(P.L. 111-148: §2001 as modified by §10201)

The health reform law includes a Medicaid eligibility maintenance of effort (MOE) requirement in which states lose access to federal financial participation under Medicaid if their eligibility standards, methodologies, or procedures under the state's Medicaid plan (including any waivers) are more restrictive than the eligibility standards, methodologies, or procedures, under a plan (or waiver) in effect as of the date of enactment (i.e., March 23, 2010). For adult populations, the MOE requirements remain in effect from the date of enactment through the date the exchanges (established by the state under Section 1311 of PPACA) are fully operational, as determined by the Secretary. For any Medicaid eligible child who is under age 19 (or such higher age as the state may have elected), the MOE will continue through September 30, 2019.[15]

The requirement to use MAGI when determining Medicaid income eligibility (as described above) will not affect compliance with the MOE requirement. States will be permitted to expand Medicaid eligibility or move populations covered under a waiver to state plan coverage at the same (or higher) eligibility level that applied under the waiver without affecting compliance.

Between January 1, 2011, and December 31, 2013, a state will be exempt from the MOE requirement for optional nonpregnant, non-disabled adult populations whose income is above 133% FPL if the state certifies to the Secretary that the state is currently experiencing a budget deficit or projects to have a budget deficit in the following state fiscal year. The state may make such certification on or after December 31, 2010. For such states, the MOE exemption will apply from the date the state submits the certification to the Secretary through December 31, 2013.

States are required to establish Medicaid income eligibility thresholds for state plan services (or waiver services) using MAGI levels that are not less than the effective income eligibility levels applicable as of the date of enactment.[16] The Secretary is permitted to waive provisions of Medicaid or CHIP to ensure that states establish income and eligibility determination systems that protect beneficiaries.

Health Care Power of Attorney

(P.L. 111-148: §2955)

Under the federal foster care program (SSA Title IV-E) a state is required to have in place a case review system for each child in foster care to, among other things, periodically review the child's status in foster care and to develop and carry out a permanency plan for the child. The case review system must ensure that a transition plan is developed for youth aging out of a state's foster care system. This usually occurs at age 18, but states can elect to cover foster care up to age 21. The plan must include specific options on housing, health insurance, education, local opportunities for mentors and continuing support services, and workforce supports and employment services. Under the Chafee Foster Care Independence Program (CFCIP; SSA §477), states receive funds to provide independent living services for youth who are expected to age out of foster care and for those who have already aged out of care. As part of their application for these funds, states must provide certain certifications regarding how the programs will be carried out. Finally, under the Stephanie Tubbs Jones Child Welfare Services Program (SSA Title IV-B, Subpart 1), states are required to develop a plan for the ongoing oversight and coordination of health care services for children in foster care. The state child welfare agency and the state agency that administers Medicaid must coordinate and collaborate in the development of this plan, and the plan must outline specific steps to ensure that children in foster care have their health care needs identified and appropriately met and that medical information for children in foster care is updated and appropriately shared.

The health reform law requires that the mandatory transition plan for a youth who is about to age out of foster care include information about the importance of designating another individual to make health care treatment decisions on behalf of the youth if he or she becomes unable to participate in these decisions and either does not have a relative who would be authorized to make these decisions under state law or does not want that relative to make those decisions. In addition, the transition plan must provide the youth with the option to execute a health care power of attorney, health care proxy, or other similar document recognized under state law.

States are required, as part of their application for CFCIP funds, to certify that foster care (or former foster care) adolescents receiving independent living services also receive education about (1) the importance of designating an individual to make health care treatment decisions for them if appropriate, (2) whether a health care power of attorney, health care proxy, or other similar document is recognized under state law, and (3) how to execute such a document if desired.

Finally, the health reform law requires that the health care oversight plan developed collaboratively between the state child welfare agency and the state Medicaid agency outline steps to ensure that the health-care related components of the transition plan for youth aging out of foster care are met. These include options for health insurance, information about a health care power of attorney, health care proxy, or other similar document recognized by state law, and the option to execute such a document. This provision is effective on October 1, 2010.

Medicaid Coverage for Former Foster Care Children

(P.L. 111-148: §2004 as modified by §10201)

Youth ages 19 or 20 may qualify for Medicaid coverage under several of the existing mandatory and optional eligibility pathways, three of which target individuals who were recently discharged from the child welfare system (i.e., Chafee Foster Care Independence Program (CFCIP)/Title IV- E, "Ribicoff" children, and youth participating in State Adoption Assistance Agreements).

The health reform law adds a second new mandatory Medicaid eligibility group to include individuals who are (1) under 26 years of age, (2) not eligible or enrolled under existing Medicaid mandatory eligibility groups (or who are described in any of the existing Medicaid mandatory eligibility groups but have income that exceeds the upper income eligibility limit established under any such group), (3) were in foster care under the responsibility of the state on the date of attaining 18 years of age (or such higher age as the state has elected), and (4) were enrolled in the Medicaid state plan or under a waiver while in such foster care. The health reform law also allows states to make "presumptive eligibility" determinations for these individuals. The provision also adds this new group of foster care youth to those exempt from enrollment in Medicaid benchmark plans (even if such individuals would also qualify for Medicaid under the new mandatory eligibility group up to 133% FPL). Benchmark and benchmark equivalent plans[17] are permitted as an alternative to regular Medicaid benefits under Section 1937 of the Social Security Act. State plan services rendered to individuals in this new mandatory eligibility group will be matched at the state's regular FMAP rate. This provision is effective as of January 1, 2014.

Protection for Recipients of Home and Community-Based Services against Spousal Impoverishment

(P.L. 111-148: §2404)

Generally, when a married individual applies to Medicaid, the combined income and assets of the couple are considered together to determine program eligibility. Medicaid law contains special rules, however, for situations in which one spouse applies for nursing home benefits under Medicaid and the other spouse does not apply for Medicaid coverage. Under these rules, referred to as spousal impoverishment protections, spouses remaining in the community do not have to meet the same stringent income and asset tests as their counterparts. By allowing them to retain higher amounts of income and assets, these protections are intended to better enable community spouses to continue residing in their homes or other community-based settings. These protections are also intended to prevent the impoverishment of those spouses who do not apply to Medicaid.

Under Medicaid law, states are required to apply spousal impoverishment protections to applicants for Medicaid nursing home care. Under prior law, they were given the option to apply these protections to applicants for certain home and community-based services (e.g., waivers under Sections 1915(c) and (d), and Section 1115 of SSA). In addition, Medicaid law previously prohibited states from applying spousal impoverishment protections to people who qualify for certain Medicaid-covered home and community-based services through an eligibility group known as medically needy. The medically needy group allows for the enrollment in Medicaid of certain persons with exceptionally high medical expenses.

The law makes three major changes to current Medicaid law. First, states are now required to apply spousal impoverishment rules to applicants who apply to Medicaid to receive certain home and community-based services (i.e., authorized under Sections 1915(c), (d), and (i) and under Section 1115 of SSA). Second, states are now required to apply spousal impoverishment protections when determining eligibility for medically needy individuals applying for certain home and community-based services. These two changes will sunset after a five-year period beginning on January 1, 2014. Third, another provision in the law allows states to use the HCBS state plan benefit option (Section 1915 (i)) as an eligibility pathway for Medicaid for certain people with long-term care needs. Spousal impoverishment rules will now apply to this new eligibility pathway. See the description of these provisions entitled "Removal of Barriers to Providing Home and Community-Based Services."

Optional Eligibility Expansions

Nonelderly, Nonpregnant Individuals with Family Income above 133% of the FPL

(P.L. 111-148: §2001 as modified by §10201)

Beginning on January 1, 2014, the law creates a new optional Medicaid eligibility category for all nonelderly, nonpregnant individuals (e.g., childless adults, and certain parents) who have income above 133% of FPL, are under age 65, and are not otherwise eligible for Medicaid under an existing mandatory eligibility group. States have the option of covering these individuals up to a maximum level specified in the Medicaid state plan (or waiver), and income eligibility for this new group will be determined based on MAGI.[18] States will be permitted to phase in Medicaid coverage to these new individuals based on their income, as long as the state does not extend coverage to (1) individuals with higher income before those with lower income, or (2) parents unless their child is enrolled in the state plan, a waiver, or in other health coverage.

State Eligibility Option for Family Planning Services

(P.L. 111-148: §2303)

"Family planning services and supplies" is a mandatory Medicaid benefit for the majority of beneficiaries of childbearing age (including minors considered to be sexually active) who desire such services and supplies. States are permitted to provide family planning services under Medicaid for populations who are not otherwise eligible for traditional Medicaid (e.g., nonpregnant, non-disabled childless adults) through special waivers.

The health reform law adds a new optional categorically needy eligibility group to Medicaid. This new group will be comprised of (1) nonpregnant individuals with income up to the highest level applicable to pregnant women covered under the Medicaid or CHIP state plan, and (2) at state option, individuals eligible under existing special waivers that provide family planning services and supplies. Benefits will be limited to family planning services and supplies and will also include related medical diagnosis and treatment services.

The new law also allows states to make a "presumptive eligibility" determination for individuals eligible for such services through the new optional eligibility group. In addition, states will not be allowed to provide Medicaid coverage through benchmark or benchmark-equivalent plans,[19] which are permissible alternatives to traditional Medicaid benefits, unless such coverage includes family planning services and supplies. This provision is effective upon enactment.

Removal of Barriers to Providing Home and Community-Based Services

(P.L. 111-148: §2402)

Under the Deficit Reduction Act of 2005 (P.L. 109-171, DRA), Congress gave states the option to extend HCBS to Medicaid beneficiaries under the HCBS state plan option (Section 1915(i) of the Social Security Act) without requiring a Secretary-approved waiver for this purpose (under Sections 1915(c) or 1115 of the Social Security Act).

Eligibility

Federal law imposes certain limitations on the characteristics of beneficiaries who may obtain these section 1915(i) services in a state. Some of these restrictions change under the health reform law. Specifically, according to prior law, this state plan option could only be extended to those Medicaid beneficiaries whose income did not exceed 150% of poverty and who met a state's needs-based criteria. The needs-based criteria, defined by states, could be no more stringent than the criteria the state uses to determine eligibility for institutional care in a nursing facility, intermediate care facility for the mentally retarded (ICF/MR), or hospital.

The new law allows states to extend access to this benefit to persons with income up to 300% of the SSI benefit rate who are receiving HCBS services under a home and community-based waiver authorized under sections 1915 (c), (d) or (e) of the SSA, or under Section 1115 off SSA (Research and Demonstration waivers). Furthermore, the law established section 1915(i) as a new optional eligibility pathway into the program. Under the new law, states may also extend full Medicaid benefits, as well as this HCBS state plan benefit, to this new eligibility group.

Targeting

Under prior law, states could target the section 1915(i) benefit to a selected population by defining a single benefit package, either broadly or narrowly, specifying the needs-based criteria for access to the benefit as expansive or narrow, and extending coverage to geographic areas that are either statewide or less than statewide. Prior law also allowed states to cap enrollment numbers and create waiting lists for those above the cap.

The new law changes the way states can target specific populations under section 1915(i). First, prior law allowed states the ability to use this benefit option to offer only a single benefit package to a single target population. The new law allows states to offer different packages of services to different target groups of beneficiaries. States can now elect to target the provision of HCBS to specific populations and to differ the type, amount, duration or scope of the benefits for each of these populations. Such elections will be for five-year periods (including an initial five-year period and five-year renewal periods). Enrollment and/or the provision of services can be phased- in, (as long as the phase-in is accomplished prior to the end of the initial five-year period).

Second, under the new law, states are no longer allowed to cap the number of persons eligible for this benefit.

Third, to help states contain enrollment, Medicaid law allows states to modify their needs-based criteria without having to obtain prior approval from the Secretary, if actual enrollment in 1915(i) exceeds states' projected enrollment, and certain other requirements are met. Under prior law, states that made their needs-based criteria more stringent were required to continue enrollment of those individuals who would become ineligible based on the new criteria for at least 12 months. Under the health reform law, such individuals will continue to be eligible until such time as the individuals no longer meets the state's former needs-based criteria.

Benefits

Under prior law, the HCBS state plan option allowed states to offer home and community-based services from a list of services contained in statute. The new law expanded that list of services to include state-selected services, other than room and board, that are approved by the Secretary.

Outreach and Enrollment Facilitation

Streamlining Procedures for Enrollment through a Health Insurance Exchange and Medicaid, CHIP, and Other Health Subsidy Programs

(P.L. 111-148: §1413)

Under the health reform law, the Secretary is required to establish a system to ensure that individuals who apply for health insurance coverage through an exchange and are found to be eligible for Medicaid or CHIP are enrolled in Medicaid or CHIP. To do this, the Secretary is required to develop and distribute a standard application form for all state health subsidy programs.

States will be permitted to develop and use their own application forms as long as they are consistent with those issued by the Secretary, and/or to use supplemental or alternative enrollment forms when household income is not used by the state in determining eligibility.

Applicants will be permitted to submit their forms online, by telephone, in person, or by mail to a state exchange, Medicaid, or CHIP program. However, states will be required to develop a secure, electronic interface for eligibility based on the standard application form. States will also be required to verify eligibility data supplied by an applicant when determining eligibility for a health subsidy program in a manner consistent with specified standards (e.g., privacy, security, accuracy, and administrative efficiency). Finally, the Secretary will be required to ensure that applicants receive notice of eligibility for state health subsidy programs, or notice when they are determined ineligible because information on their application is inconsistent with electronic verification data, or is otherwise insufficient to determine eligibility. This provision is effective January 1, 2014.

Enrollment Simplification and Coordination with State Health Insurance Exchanges

(P.L. 111-148: §2201)

As a condition of the Medicaid state plan and receipt of any federal financial assistance after January 1, 2014, the health reform law requires states to meet the following requirements:

1. States will be required to establish procedures for
   - enabling individuals to apply for, or renew enrollment in, Medicaid or CHIP through an internet website allowing electronic signatures;
   - enrolling individuals who are identified by an exchange as being eligible for Medicaid or CHIP, without any further determination by the state;
   - ensuring that individuals who apply for Medicaid and/or CHIP but are determined ineligible for either program are screened for enrollment eligibility in qualified plans offered through the exchanges, and if applicable, obtain premium assistance for such coverage without having to submit an additional or separate application;
   - ensuring that the state Medicaid agency, CHIP agency, and the exchanges utilize a secure electronic interface that allows for eligibility determinations and enrollment in Medicaid, CHIP or premium assistance for a qualified plan as appropriate;
   - ensuring that Medicaid and/or CHIP enrollees who are also enrolled in qualified health benefits plan through the exchanges are provided Medicaid medical assistance and/or CHIP child health assistance that is coordinated with the exchange coverage, including services related to Early and Periodic Screening, Diagnostic and Treatment (EPSDT); and
   - conduct outreach and enrollment of vulnerable populations such as unaccompanied homeless youth, racial and ethnic minorities, and individuals with HIV/AIDS;
2. The state Medicaid and CHIP agencies may enter into an agreement with the exchanges under which each agency may determine whether a state resident is eligible for premium assistance for the purchase of a qualified health benefits plan under an exchange, so long as the agreement meets specified requirements to reduce administrative costs, eligibility errors, and disruptions in coverage;
3. The Medicaid and CHIP agency will be required to comply with the requirements for the system established under § 1413 (relating to streamlined procedures for enrollment through exchanges, Medicaid and CHIP); and
4. States are required to establish a website (not later than January 1, 2014) that links Medicaid to the state exchanges.

Permitting Hospitals to Make Presumptive Eligibility Determinations for All Medicaid Eligible Populations

(P.L. 111-148: §2202)

Under current law, states may enroll certain groups (i.e., children, pregnant women, and certain women with breast and cervical cancer) for a limited period of time before completed Medicaid applications are filed and processed, based on a preliminary determination by a Medicaid provider of likely Medicaid eligibility. Such individuals must then formally apply for coverage within a certain timeframe to continue receiving Medicaid benefits. Presumptive eligibility begins on the date a qualified Medicaid provider determines that the applicant appears to meet eligibility criteria and ends on the earlier of (1) the date on which a formal determination is made regarding the individual's application for Medicaid, or (2) in the case of an individual who fails to apply for Medicaid following the presumptive eligibility determination, the last day of the month following the month in which presumptive eligibility begins.

The health reform law allows states to permit all hospitals that participate in Medicaid to make presumptive eligibility determinations, based on a preliminary determination of likely Medicaid eligibility, for all Medicaid eligible populations. Such preliminary eligibility determinations are subject to guidance established by the Secretary and will need to follow the same requirements as currently apply to presumptive eligibility (i.e., for children, pregnant women, and certain women with breast or cervical cancer) regardless of whether the state has opted to extend presumptive eligibility to any of these groups. States are permitted to enroll such individuals for a limited period of time before completed Medicaid applications are filed and processed. Beneficiary claims submitted during the period of presumptive eligibility will not be included among those reviewed to determine if improper payments were made based on errors in the state agency's eligibility determinations. The provision is effective on January 1, 2014.

New Reporting Requirements

(P.L. 111-148: §2001 as modified by §10201)

The health reform law requires states to report on changes in Medicaid enrollment beginning January 2015, and every year thereafter. As a part of these reporting requirements, states must submit enrollment estimates of the total number of "newly enrolled" individuals by fiscal year, disaggregated by

(1) children, (2) parents, (3) nonpregnant childless adults, (4) disabled individuals, (5) elderly individuals, and (6) such other categories or sub-categories of individuals eligible for Medicaid as the Secretary may require. States are also required to report on their outreach and enrollment processes, and any other data reporting specified by the Secretary to monitor enrollment and retention in Medicaid. The Secretary is required to submit a report to the appropriate committees of Congress (beginning in April 2015 and every year thereafter) on total new enrollment in Medicaid by state, as well as recommendations for improving Medicaid enrollment.

Benefits

Traditional Medicaid benefits are identified in federal statute and regulations, and include a wide range of acute and long-term care services and supplies. Additional benefits include premium payments for coverage provided through Medicaid managed care arrangements or for employer-sponsored insurance, and Medicare premium and cost-sharing support for persons dually eligible for both Medicare and Medicaid.

Modifications to DRA Benchmark and Benchmark-Equivalent Coverage

(P.L. 111-148: §2001(c) and §2303(c))

As an alternative to traditional benefits, the Deficit Reduction Act (DRA; P.L. 109-171) gave states the option to provide Medicaid to state-specified groups through enrollment in benchmark and benchmark-equivalent coverage similar to coverage available under the State Children's Health Insurance Program (CHIP). Benchmark coverage includes (1) the Blue Cross/Blue Shield standard plan option under the Federal Employees Health Benefits Program (FEHBP), (2) the coverage generally available to state employees, (3) the coverage offered by the largest commercial HMO in the state, and (4) Secretary-approved coverage appropriate for the target population. In general, benchmark and benchmark-equivalent coverage may be less generous than traditional Medicaid, but there are some requirements described below, that might make it more generous than private insurance. It can be provided in sub-state areas, and can be limited to subpopulations of Medicaid beneficiaries. As noted previously, such benefit packages will be required for the newly eligible population with income below 133% FPL, with exemptions from mandatory enrollment for certain subgroups (e.g., those with special needs).

Prior to PPACA, benchmark-equivalent coverage included certain basic benefits (i.e., inpatient and outpatient hospital services, physician services, lab/x-ray, well-child care including immunizations, and other appropriate preventive services designated by the Secretary), and also included at least 75% of the actuarial value of available coverage under the selected benchmark option for specific additional benefits (i.e., prescription drugs, mental health services, vision care and hearing services). Benchmark and benchmark-equivalent coverage must include Early and Periodic Screening, Diagnostic and Treatment (EPSDT) services (whether provided by the issuer of such coverage or otherwise) as well as access to services provided by rural health clinics and federally qualified health centers. Finally, a recent CMS regulation[20] requires that states ensure medically necessary transportation to and from providers when such transportation is not a covered benefit under both benchmark and benchmark-equivalent plans.

According to the recent CMS regulation noted previously, some states have experience with benchmark benefits under Medicaid. CMS has approved 10 benchmark packages, of which 8 are classified as Secretary-approved coverage. Most offer traditional state plan benefits plus additional services such as preventive care, personal assistance services, and disease management services.

The health reform law modifies benchmark and benchmark-equivalent benefit packages available under Medicaid. All such plans must include family planning services and supplies as of the date of enactment of PPACA (March 23, 2010). Such packages will also be required to provide at least essential benefits as of January 1, 2014. Essential health benefits[21] will include at least (1) ambulatory patient services, (2) emergency services, (3) hospitalization, (4) maternity and newborn care, (5) mental health and substance use disorder services, including behavioral health treatment, (6) prescription drugs, (7) rehabilitative and habilitative services and devices, (8) laboratory services, (9) preventive and wellness services and chronic disease management, and (10) pediatric services, including oral and vision care. For Medicaid benchmark-equivalent plans, prescription drugs and mental health services will be added to the list of basic services that must be covered under the plan.

In the case of any benchmark benefit package or benchmark-equivalent coverage offered by an entity that is not a Medicaid managed care plan and that provides both medical and surgical benefits and mental health or substance use disorder benefits, such entity will be required to ensure that the financial requirements and treatment limitations applicable to such benefits comply with the mental health services parity requirements of Section 2705(a) of the Public Health Service Act in the same manner as these requirements apply to a group health plan. Coverage of EPSDT services will be deemed to meet the mental health services parity requirement.

Premium Assistance

(P.L. 111-148: §2003 as modified by §10203(b))

The health reform law also permits states to offer premium assistance with wrap-around benefits (i.e., Medicaid covered services not included in employer plans) to Medicaid eligible individuals when it is cost-effective to do so. Premium assistance plans are determined cost effective if (1) the amount of expenditures under the state CHIP plan (including administrative costs) that the state would have made to provide comparable coverage of the children (or families) involved, or (2) the aggregate amount of expenditures that the state would have made under CHIP (including administrative expenses) for providing coverage under the plan for all such children (or families).[22] However, beneficiaries will not be required to apply for enrollment in employer plans, and individuals will be permitted to disenroll from such plans at any time. In addition, states will be required to pay premiums and cost-sharing in excess of amounts permitted under current Medicaid program rules (i.e., nominal amounts specified in regulations and inflation adjusted over time, or higher amounts authorized in P.L. 109-171, the DRA). These provisions are effective as if included in P.L. 111-3 (CHIPRA).

Birthing Centers

(P.L. 111-148: §2301)

The health reform law requires Medicaid coverage of care provided in free-standing birthing centers. In addition, states will be required to separately pay providers administering prenatal, labor and delivery or postpartum care in freestanding birthing centers, such as nurse midwives and birth attendants, as deemed appropriate by the Secretary. This provision is effective on the date of enactment (except if state legislation is required, in which case additional time for compliance is permitted).

Optional Adult (and Child) Preventive Care

(P.L. 111-148: §4106)

Currently, most Medicaid beneficiaries under age 21 are entitled to mandatory EPSDT services, which include well-child visits, immunizations, laboratory tests, as well as vision, dental, and hearing screening services at regular intervals. Also under prior law, some preventive services may be available to Medicaid adults (persons age 21 and over) through an optional benefit covering "other diagnostic, screening, preventive and rehabilitative services." Under P.L. 111- 148, the previously existing Medicaid option to provide "other diagnostic, screening, preventive, and rehabilitation services" will be explicitly expanded to include:

1. *any* clinical preventive services recommended (i.e., assigned a grade of A or B) by the United States Preventive Services Task Force (USPSTF), including preventive services that may already be coverable under the mandatory EPSDT benefit for persons under age 21, and
2. *adult* immunizations recommended by the Advisory Committee on Immunization Practices (ACIP) and their administration.

For purposes of this provision, beginning January 2013, states will receive a one percentage point increase in their FMAP for these services when they are covered with no cost-sharing for beneficiaries.

Smoking Cessation Services for Pregnant Women

(P.L. 111-148: §4107)

Pregnancy-related services are a mandatory benefit for the majority of Medicaid beneficiaries. Those services include prenatal, delivery, postpartum care, family planning services, as well as services to ameliorate conditions that complicate pregnancy (e.g., those that threaten the carrying of the fetus to full-term or the safe delivery of the fetus). P.L. 111-148 adds counseling and pharmacotherapy to promote cessation of tobacco use by pregnant women as a mandatory benefit under Medicaid beginning on October 1, 2010. Such coverage includes prescription and nonprescription tobacco cessation agents approved by the Food and Drug Administration (FDA). Services will be limited to those recommended for pregnant women in *Treating Tobacco Use and Dependence: 2008 Update: A Clinical Practice Guideline* (and if applicable, as subsequently modified), as well as other related tobacco cessation services designated by the Secretary.[23] Cost-sharing for such counseling and pharmacotherapy for pregnant women will be prohibited, as is true for other pregnancy-related services under Medicaid. Beginning January 1, 2013, states will receive a one percentage point increase in their regular FMAP for these smoking cessation services for pregnant women if they elect to cover the new optional adult preventive care benefit (described above).

Scope of Coverage for Children Receiving Hospice Care

(P.L. 111-148: §2302)

States have the option to offer hospice services under Medicaid and nearly all states do so. Medicaid beneficiaries who elect to receive such services must waive the right to all other services related to the individual's diagnosis of a terminal illness or condition, including treatment. PPACA allows payment for services provided to Medicaid children (defined by the state) who have voluntarily elected to receive hospice services, without foregoing coverage of and payment for other services to treat their terminal illness. This provision also applies to CHIP, and is effective upon enactment.

Community First Choice Option

(P.L. 111-148: §2401 and P.L. 111-152: §1205)

Personal care attendants provide assistance with activities of daily living (ADL) and/or instrumental activities of daily living (IADL) to individuals with a significant disability. ADLs generally refer to eating, bathing and showering, using the toilet, dressing, walking across a small room, and transferring (getting in or out of a bed or chair). IADLs include preparing meals, managing money, shopping for groceries or personal items, performing housework, using a telephone, among others. Under current law, states are permitted to cover personal care services, including personal care attendant services, under a variety of optional statutory authorities such as (1) the personal care state plan benefit; (2) self-directed personal care state plan benefit; (3) home and community-based services state plan benefit (Section 1915(i)); (4) HCBS Waiver (Sections 1915(c)(d)(e)); and (5) Research and Demonstration Waivers (Section 1115). Although states have significant flexibility to determine the amount and scope of these benefits, each statutory authority includes a unique set of rules limiting the way in which a state may extend this benefit to Medicaid beneficiaries.

The health reform law allows states to offer consumer-directed personal care attendant services under a new statuary authority, and provides an increased match rate for doing so of 6 percentage points. Beginning October 1, 2011, states can offer home and community-based attendant services as an optional benefit to Medicaid beneficiaries whose income does not exceed 150% of the federal poverty level, or if greater, the income level applicable for an individual who has been determined to require the level of care offered in a hospital, nursing facility, or intermediate care facility for the mentally retarded (ICF/MR), or an institution for mental disease.

Services offered under this benefit option will include, among others, home and community- based attendant services and supports to assist eligible individuals in accomplishing ADLs, IADLs, and health-related tasks. Such services must be delivered under a person-centered plan of care in which attendants are selected, managed, and dismissed by the individual (or his or her representative). Services and supports may also include expenditures for transition costs, such as from a nursing home to the community. Such costs might include first month's rent and utilities, bedding, and basic kitchen supplies, among others. Further, attendants must be qualified to deliver such services and may include family members (as defined by the Secretary).

To obtain approval from the Secretary to offer this benefit, states must (1) collaborate with a state-established Development and Implementation Council; (2) provide these services on a statewide basis and in the most integrated setting, as is deemed appropriate to meet the needs of the individual; (3) in the first full fiscal year of operation, maintain or exceed the preceding fiscal year's level of state Medicaid expenditures for individuals with disabilities or elderly individuals; and (4) establish and maintain a comprehensive, continuous quality assurance system, among other requirements.

No later than December 31, 2013, the Secretary must submit to Congress an interim report on the findings of an evaluation. A final report on the community-based attendant services and supports option is due to Congress by December 31, 2015.

State Option to Provide Health Homes for Enrollees with Chronic Conditions

(P.L. 111-148: §2703)

A health home, also referred to as medical home, provides patients with access to a primary care medical provider, and is thought to ultimately improve patient health outcomes. In theory, a medical home would provide participants with access to a personal primary care physician, or specialist, with an office care team, who would coordinate and facilitate care. Physician-guided, patient-centered care is expected to enhance patient adherence to recommended treatment and avoid (1) hospitalizations, unnecessary office visits, tests, and procedures; (2) use of expensive technology or biologicals when less expensive tests or treatments are equally effective; and (3) patient safety risks inherent in inconsistent treatment decisions. In practice, medical homes are physicians offices that, in exchange for a fee, provide care coordination and management to patients.

PPACA establishes a new Medicaid state plan option, beginning January 1, 2011, under which certain Medicaid enrollees with chronic conditions could designate a health home, as defined by the Secretary.

In states that choose to offer this benefit option, individuals with chronic conditions will be eligible. For the purpose of this benefit, chronic conditions include a mental health condition, a substance abuse disorder, asthma, diabetes, heart disease, and a Body Mass Index over 25 (overweight). To be eligible, the patient would have, at a minimum, (1) at least two chronic conditions; (2) one chronic condition and be at risk of having a second chronic condition; or (3) one serious and persistent mental health condition. Higher eligibility requirements, however, can be established by the Secretary.

To assemble their health home, patients can designate providers, teams of health care professionals operating with providers, or health teams. A designated provider can be a physician, clinical practice or clinical group practice, rural clinic, community health center, community mental health center, home health agency, pediatrician, gynecologist, obstetrician or other qualified entity, as determined by the state and approved by the Secretary. To be qualified, the provider must offer services including comprehensive care management, care coordination, health promotion, transitional care, patient and family support, referral to community and social support services, and use of health information technology. In all cases, the Secretary will establish the standards for qualification.

States will be reimbursed for payments by the federal government at a 90% FMAP for the first eight fiscal quarters. States that choose to implement it will receive assistance according to their regular FMAP after the first eight fiscal year quarters. States can use a variety of payment schedules to reimburse providers. In addition, the state plan must provide referrals from hospitals to providers; coordination across substance abuse, mental health, and other services; various monitoring arrangements; and reports on the quality of the health home option.

Beginning January 1, 2011, the Secretary may award planning grants to the states for developing their health home programs. Each state must match the federal contribution using its normal matching rate. The total payments made to the states will not exceed $25 million.

The Secretary is required to use an independent entity to evaluate this program. The evaluation will focus on whether the program reduces hospital admissions, emergency room visits, and admissions to skilled nursing facilities. The evaluation will first be presented to the Secretary and then to Congress by January 1, 2017. By January 1, 2014, however, the Secretary must survey the states that have participated in this program, and report to Congress on a variety of topics, including the program's effects on hospital admission rates, chronic disease management, coordination of care for individuals with chronic conditions, assessment of quality improvements, estimates of cost savings, and other topics.

Changes to Existing Medicaid Benefits

Removal of Barriers to Providing Home and Community-Based Services

(P.L. 111-148: §2402)

See "Eligibility" section for provision description.

Clarification of The Definition of Medical Assistance

(P.L. 111-148: §2304)

The term "medical assistance" means payment of part or all of the cost of care and services identified in federal statute. This term is repeated throughout Title XIX, Grants to States for Medical Assistance Programs, of the SSA. PPACA clarifies that "medical assistance" encompasses both payment for services provided and the services themselves. This provision is effective upon enactment.

Financing

Financing for Medicaid is shared by the federal government and the states. The federal share for most Medicaid expenses for benefits is determined by the federal medical assistance percentage (FMAP). FMAP rates are based on a formula that provides higher federal reimbursement to states with lower per capita income relative to the national average (and vice versa). FMAPs have a statutory minimum of 50% and a maximum of 83%, although some Medicaid services receive a higher federal match rate. FY2010 FMAPs ranged from a high of 75.67% in Mississippi to a low of 50.00% in 10 other states. In February 2009, with passage of the American Recovery and Reinvestment Act of 2009 (ARRA), states received temporary enhanced FMAP rates for nine quarters beginning with the first quarter of FY2009 and running through the first quarter of FY2011 (December 31, 2010).

State expenditures to administer Medicaid programs are generally matched by federal funding at 50%. Federal matching rates for administrative expenditures are the same for all states, although some activities are matched at higher rates.

Payments to States

Additional Federal Financial Assistance under Health Reform

(P.L. 111-148: §2001 as modified by §10201, and P.L. 111-152: §1201 and §1202)

Federal Funding for Existing Eligibility Groups

Beginning in 2014, expansion states, (those that, as of March 23, 2010, offered full package of health benefits for parents and childless adults up to at least 100% FPL—see provision definitions below) will get an increased FMAP for childless adults who qualify under the new Medicaid eligibility pathway for people up to 133% FPL but do not meet the definition of "newly eligible" as discussed below. The increase will be a certain percentage (i.e., "transition percentage")[24] of the difference between the state's regular FMAP and the FMAP it receives for "newly eligibles" as illustrated in the last row of **Table 1**.

Between January 1, 2014, and December 31, 2015, specified expansion states will receive an increase in their regular FMAP rate of 2.2 percentage points with respect to amounts expended for medical assistance for individuals who are *not* "newly eligible" (as defined below). To be eligible, a state must (1) be an "expansion state" (as defined below), (2) be determined by the Secretary to be a state that would not receive additional federal matching funds for "newly eligible" individuals, and (3) not have been granted Secretary approval to divert a portion of such state's disproportionate share hospitals (DSH) allotment for the purpose of providing medical assistance or other health benefits coverage under a waiver in effect on July 2009. The FMAP increase described in this provision will not apply to (1) Disproportionate Share Hospital payments, (2) payments under CHIP, and (3) payments under Medicaid that are based on the CHIP enhanced FMAP rate. The only state that appears to qualify for the 2.2 percentage point increase is Vermont.

Federal Funding for "Newly Eligible" Populations

Under the health reform law, states will receive 100% FMAP for the cost of providing benchmark or benchmark-equivalent coverage to "newly eligible" individuals (defined for the purposes of this subsection below), from 2014 through 2016.[25] For "newly eligible" individuals, the FMAP rate will be 95% in 2017, 94% in 2018, 93% in 2019, and 90% afterward (see **Table 1**). Finally, in the case of a state that requires a political subdivision within the state to contribute the nonfederal share of expenditures, such state would not be eligible for an increase in its FMAP (under this provision or under the FMAP increases provided under the American Recovery and Reinvestment Act of 2009) if it requires that political subdivisions pay a greater percentage of the non-federal share of expenditures (including expenditures for DSH) than amounts that would have been required as of December 31, 2009. Voluntary contributions are not considered "required" contributions.

For the purposes of this financing provision:

- "Newly eligible" individuals are defined as nonelderly, nonpregnant individuals with family income below 133% FPL who (1) are not under the age of 19 (or such higher age as the state may have elected), and (2) are not eligible under the state plan (or a waiver) for full Medicaid state plan benefits or for Medicaid benchmark or benchmark-equivalent coverage, or are eligible but not enrolled (or are on a waiting list) in such coverage as of December 1, 2009.

- Full Medicaid state plan benefits are defined as medical assistance that includes all services of the same amount, duration, and scope, or that is determined by the Secretary to be substantially equivalent to the Medicaid state plan services available to categorically eligible mandatory coverage groups.
- "Expansion states" are defined as states (as of March 23, 2010) that had health benefits coverage (that includes inpatient hospital services) for parents and nonpregnant childless adults with income of at least 100% FPL. Such health benefits coverage may not be based on employer coverage or employment. While health benefits coverage may be less comprehensive than Medicaid, the law requires such coverage to be more than (1) premium assistance, (2) hospital-only benefits, (3) a high deductible health plan, or (4) alternative benefits under a demonstration program authorized under Section 1938 (health opportunity accounts); and

Incentives for States to Offer Home and Community-Based Services as a Long-Term Care Alternative to Nursing Homes

(P.L. 111-148: §10202)

Under Medicaid, states make available a broad range of institutional and home and community-based long-term care services to certain Medicaid enrollees. States are required to offer only some of these services. For those services that are offered, states define them differently, using criteria that place limits on the amount, duration, and scope of the benefits. States also restrict benefits to just those persons who demonstrate medical necessity for the benefit. Under Medicaid, institutional services are generally defined as care provided in nursing facilities, intermediate care facilities for people with mental retardation (ICFs/MR), inpatient hospital services and institutions for mental diseases (IMDs). Home and community-based services are generally defined as long-term care services offered under Medicaid's mandatory home health state plan benefit, and a variety of optional state plan benefits, including personal care, case management or targeted case management, respiratory care for persons who are ventilator-dependent, Program of All-inclusive Care for the Elderly (PACE), transportation, home and community-based services (under section 1915(i) of the Social Security Act), and Medicaid home and community-based 1915(c) and (d) waivers.

The health reform law allows qualifying states to receive bonus payments for increasing their share of Medicaid long-term care spending on HCBS and reducing their share of Medicaid LTC spending on institutional care. To receive payments, states will be required to meet certain target- spending percentages. If the state's spending on home and community-based services in FY2009 is less than 25%, the state must achieve a 25% target on HCBS by October 1, 2015, to receive bonus payments. Such states will receive an FMAP increase of 5 percentage points on eligible medical assistance payments. Other states will be required to reach a target of 50% by October 1, 2015, to qualify for payments. These states will receive an FMAP increase of 2 percentage points for eligible payments. In no case may the aggregate amount of payments made by the Secretary to states exceed $3 billion. The balancing incentive period begins October 1, 2011, and ends on September 30, 2015.

To receive incentive payments, a state is required to submit an application that includes a proposed budget detailing the state's plan to expand and diversify medical assistance for non- institutionally based long-term care services and supports during the balancing incentive period and to achieve the target spending percentage applicable to the state. For states proposing to expand the Section 1915(i) benefit, the application must include a description of the state's election to increase the eligibility level above 150% of the FPL to a percentage not exceeding 300% of the SSI benefit rate. Regarding a state's structural changes, the application must include a description of the new or expanded offerings of those services that the state will provide and the projected costs of such services.

States must also collect data from providers and others on services, quality, and outcomes measures.

To qualify for payments, states may not apply more restrictive eligibility standards, methodologies, or procedures then were in effect on December 31, 2010. In addition, states must agree to use additional incentive payments for new or expanded offerings of HCBS services under Medicaid. Further, states must agree to implement the following:

Table 1. Federal Medicaid Medical Assistance Payment (FMAP) Rates for Required Medicaid Expansions, Beginning 2014

	2014	2015	2016	2017	2018	2019	2020+
"Newly eligible" adults in all states	100%	100%	100%	95%	94%	93%	90%
Previously eligible childless adults in expansion states	75%-90%	80%-92%	85%-94%	86%-92%	90%-92.6%	93%	90%

Source: Table prepared by CRS Specialist in Health Care Financing, Chris L. Peterson, based on provisions in P.L. 111-148, as amended by P.L. 111-152.

Notes: "Expansion states" are those that, as of the date of PPACA's enactment (March 23, 201 0), had covered parents and childless adults up to 100% FPL. Although the Department of Health and Human Services will make the official determination of which states will be considered "expansion states" under PPACA and the HCERA, existing Medicaid eligibility information suggests that 11 states and the District of Columbia meet this definition including Arizona, Delaware, Hawaii, Maine, Massachusetts, Minnesota, New York, Pennsylvania, Vermont, Washington, and Wisconsin. The FMAP ranges for previously eligible childless adults (i.e., individuals who would have been previously eligible for full benefit coverage in the state) under PPACA and HCERA represent the potential FMAP rate based on regular FMAPs ranging from the statutory minimum (50%) to 80%. (The highest regular FMAP since 2000 was 77.08%, although FMAPs are permitted statutorily to go to 83%.)

- **no wrong door-single entry point system**—a statewide system enabling consumers to access all long-term care services through an agency, organization, coordinated network, or portal;
- **conflict-free case management services**—to develop a service plan, arrange for services, support the beneficiary (and, if appropriate, the caregiver) in directing his or her services, and conduct ongoing monitoring; and
- **core standardized assessment**—instruments for determining eligibility for non-institutionally based long-term care services, uniformly used across the state, to determine the beneficiary's needs for training, support services, medical care, transportation, and other services, and develop an individual service plan.

Disproportionate Share Hospital Payments

(P.L. 111-148: §2551 as modified by §10201(e); P.L. 111-152: §1203)

Under Medicaid, states are required to make disproportionate share hospital (DSH) adjustments to the payment rates of hospitals treating large numbers of low-income and Medicaid patients. The DSH provision is intended to recognize the disadvantaged situation of those hospitals. States must define, in their state Medicaid plans, hospitals that qualify as DSH hospitals and their DSH payment formulas. DSH hospitals must include at least all hospitals meeting minimum criteria and may not include hospitals that have a Medicaid utilization rate below 1%. The DSH payment formula also must meet minimum criteria, and DSH payments for any specific hospital cannot exceed a hospital-specific cap based on the unreimbursed costs of providing hospital services to Medicaid and uninsured patients.

In claiming federal DSH matching dollars, states cannot exceed their state-specific allotment amounts, calculated for each state based on a statutory formula. In determining these allotments for states, special rules apply to "low DSH states" (those in which total DSH payments for FY2000 were less than 3% of the state's total Medicaid spending on benefits). For low DSH states for FY2004 through FY2008, the allotment for each of these years was equal to 16% more than the prior year's amount. For years beginning in FY2009, DSH allotments for all states are equal to the prior year amount increased by the change in the consumer price index for all urban consumers (CPI-U). For FY2009, federal DSH allotments across states and the District of Columbia totaled to nearly $10.6 billion. Provisions under ARRA provided additional temporary DSH funding for states that increases total federal DSH allotments to nearly $10.9 billion.

P.L. 111-152 requires the Secretary to make aggregate reductions in Medicaid DSH allotments equal to $500 million in FY2014, $600 million in FY2015, $600 million in FY2016, $1.8 billion in FY2017, $5.0 billion in FY2018, $5.6 billion in FY2019, and $4.0 billion in FY2020.

To achieve these aggregate reductions, the Secretary will be required to:

1. impose the largest percentage reduction on states that
   - have the lowest percentage of uninsured individuals (determined on the basis of data from the Bureau of the Census, audited hospital cost reports, and other information likely to yield accurate data) during the most recent fiscal year with available data, or
   - do not target their DSH payments to hospitals with high volumes of Medicaid patients, and hospitals that have high levels of uncompensated care (excluding bad debt);
2. impose a smaller percentage reduction on low DSH states; and

3. take into account the extent to which the DSH allotment for a state was included in the budget neutrality calculation for a coverage expansion approved under a section 1115 waiver as of July 31, 2009.

Under prior law, two states that operate their Medicaid programs through waivers—Tennessee and Hawaii—have special statutory arrangements relating to their specific DSH allotments. Tennessee's allotment amount was set at $30 million for each of fiscal years 2009 through 2011. Under PPACA, Medicaid DSH allotments will be set at $47.2 million for FY2012 and $53.1 million for FY2013 for Tennessee.

Hawaii's DSH allotment was set at $10 million for each of fiscal years 2009 through 2011. Under PPACA, Hawaii's DSH allotment will also be set at $10 million for FY2012. For FY2013 forward, Hawaii's annual DSH allotment will be increased in the same manner applicable to low DSH states (i.e., adjusted by the percentage change in the Consumer Price Index for All Urban Consumers, CPI-U, from year to year). The provision also prohibits the Secretary from imposing a limit on payments made to hospitals under Hawaii's QUEST Section 1115 demonstration project, except to the extent necessary to ensure that a hospital does not receive payments in excess of its hospital specific cap, or that payments do not exceed the amount that the Secretary determines is equal to the federal share of DSH within the budget neutrality provision of the QUEST demonstration project.

Special FMAP Adjustment for States Recovering from a Major Disaster

(P.L. 111-148: §2006)

In recent years, the fiscal situation of the states has focused attention on the size of the state's share of Medicaid expenditures, as well as changes in the federal share of those expenditures. For instance, under the Jobs and Growth Tax Relief Reconciliation Act of 2003 (P.L. 108-27), all states and the District of Columbia received a temporary increase in Medicaid FMAPs for the last two quarters of FY2003 and the first three quarters of FY2004 as part of a fiscal relief package. Medicaid FMAPs for the last two quarters of FY2003 and the first three quarters of FY2004 were held harmless from annual declines and were increased by an additional 2.95 percentage points, as long as states met certain other requirements. States' FMAP rates returned to normal for the last quarter of FY2004 and continued until the ARRA enhanced rates in FY2009.

During the most recent recession, Congress provided states additional economic stimulus funding, including enhanced FMAP rates, when ARRA became law in February 2009.[26] States, the District of Columbia and the territories, received enhanced FMAP rates under ARRA for the recession period which began with the first quarter of FY2009 and continues through the first quarter of FY2011 (December 31, 2010). Under ARRA, all states are held harmless from declines in their normal FMAP rates beginning with FY2008 and continuing through the recession period. States and the District of Columbia receive an across-the-board FMAP increase of 6.2 percentage points, and qualifying states receive an additional unemployment-related increase. ARRA allowed each territory a one time choice between an FMAP increase of 6.2 percentage points along with a 15% increase in its spending cap, or its regular FMAP along with a 30% increase in its spending cap. All territories chose the 30% spending cap increase. In addition, DRA included provisions to exclude certain Hurricane Katrina evacuees and their incomes from FMAP calculations, prevent Alaska's FY2006-FY2007 FMAPs from falling below the state's FY2005 level, and provide $2 billion to help pay for (among other things) the state share of certain Katrina-related Medicaid and CHIP costs.

PPACA Section 2006 provides for additional FMAP above the regular FMAP levels for qualifying "disaster-recovery FMAP adjustment" states once the ARRA adjustment is no longer in effect (January 1, 2011). To qualify for this adjustment, states must (1) have been declared by the President as a major disaster area during the preceding seven fiscal years under Sec. 401 of the Stafford Act for which every county or parish was determined to merit federal assistance, and (2) for FY2011, have its regular FMAP be at least three percentage points lower than the state's highest regular FMAP since FY2008 (excluding the ARRA 6.2-point and unemployment adjustments). Only three states will meet the second requirement—Louisiana (8.86 points), Hawaii (4.71 points), and North Dakota (3.40 points). Of those, only Louisiana meets the first requirement. For the portion of FY2011 not in the ARRA recession adjustment period (i.e., after December 31, 2010), PPACA will provide Louisiana with an FMAP of 68.04% (rather than the currently slated 63.6 1%). The FMAP of 68.04% will be 13.4-point drop from its latest ARRA FMAP, which is still the second-largest drop (behind Hawaii's 15.6-point drop) from the latest ARRA-adjusted FMAPs.[27] State eligibility for disaster relief would be re-determined annually. In the future, other states may qualify for the special disaster relief FMAP increase if they meet both requirements. This Section is effective January 1, 2011.

Payments to the Territories

(P.L. 111-148: §2005 as modified by §10201; P.L. 111-152: §1204)

Five territories (American Samoa, Guam, the Northern Mariana Islands, Puerto Rico, and the U.S. Virgin Islands) operate Medicaid programs under rules that differ from those applicable to the states and the District of Columbia (hereinafter referred to as the states for the purposes of this provision). The territories are not required to cover the same eligibility groups, and they use different financial standards (income and asset tests) in determining eligibility compared to the states. For example, states must cover certain mandatory groups such as pregnant women, children, and qualified Medicare beneficiaries, but for the territories, these groups are optional. In addition, Medicaid programs in the territories are subject to annual federal spending caps. All five territories typically exhaust their caps prior to the end of the fiscal year. Once the cap is reached, the territories assume the full costs of Medicaid services or, in some instances, may suspend services or cease payments to providers until the next fiscal year. Finally, under prior law, the FMAP for all the territories was set at 50%.

The health reform law permits the territories to establish exchanges (in accordance with the exchange-related provisions in PPACA), not later than October 13, 2013. Out of funds not otherwise appropriated, $1.0 billion is appropriated for the period between 2014 and 2019 for the purpose of providing premium and cost-sharing assistance to residents of the territories to obtain health insurance coverage through the exchanges. Of this amount, the Secretary is to allocate $925 million for Puerto Rico, and a portion (as specified by the Secretary) of the remaining $75 million for any other territory that chooses establish exchanges. Under this provision, territories are to be treated as states and required to structure their exchanges in a manner so there is no gap in assistance between individuals eligible for Medicaid and those eligible for premium and cost sharing assistance.

Territories that do not elect to establish a exchanges as of the specified date are entitled to an increase in their existing Medicaid funding caps. For the period between July 1, 2011, and September 30, 2019, $6.3 billion in total additional payments are available for distribution among each territory in an amount that is proportional to the capped amounts available to the territories under current law. The FMAP for all the territories will be increased from 50% to 55% beginning on July 1, 2011. Current law rules regarding funds spent on specified administrative activities will apply, and the provision is effective July 1, 2011.

Payments for Primary Care Providers

(P.L. 111-152: §1202)

State Medicaid plans must provide methods and procedures to assure that payments are consistent with efficiency, economy, and quality of care. They must also be sufficient to enlist enough providers so that care and services are available at least to the extent that such care is available to the general population in the geographic area. Additional requirements regarding payment rates under Medicaid apply to inpatient hospital and long-term care facility services. However, within these guidelines, states have considerable flexibility to set provider reimbursement rates independent of any national baseline or reference.

Under HCERA (P.L. 111-152), states will be required to set Medicaid payments for primary care services [i.e., evaluation and management (E&M) services defined by Medicare as of December 31, 2009, and as subsequently modified by the Secretary, and services related to immunization administration for vaccines and toxoids] relative to Medicare payment rates. Primary care services furnished in 2013 and 2014 by a physician with a primary specialty designation of family medicine, general internal medicine, or pediatric medicine will be paid at the Medicare rate for these services or higher.

With respect to Medicaid managed care, P.L. 111-152 also requires that, in the case of E&M services, these new payment rates will apply, regardless of the manner in which such payments are made, including in the form of capitation or partial capitation (e.g., payments made on a "per member per month" basis, rather than for each specific unit of service delivered).

For services furnished in 2013 and 2014, the federal government will fully finance the portion of primary care service payments by which the new minimum payment rates exceed the state's existing payment rates as of July 1, 2009. That is, the federal FMAP for the additional costs will equal 100% in those two years.

Payments to Providers for Health-Care Acquired Conditions

(P.L. 111-148: §2702)

Medicare uses a prospective payment system (PPS) to reimburse hospitals for inpatient care. Medicare's PPS classifies each hospital admission into severity adjusted diagnosis-related groups (MS-DRG) based on the patient's diagnosis and procedures performed.

The DRA required the Secretary to initiate a hospital-acquired condition (HAC) program.[28] Beginning October 1, 2008, when Medicare patients were admitted with certain HACs identified by the Secretary, then the presence of these conditions at admission would allow the hospital to receive an additional MS-DRG payment if these conditions affected the patient's treatment. However, if a patient did not have one of the HACs at admission, but acquired one during their stay, then the hospital could not receive an additional MS-DRG payment. In addition to the HAC policy, CMS issued three national coverage determinations in January 2009 that prohibited Medicare from reimbursing hospitals for certain serious preventable medical care errors. [29] Medicaid was not covered by DRA's HAC policy or CMS's national coverage decisions.

Although Medicaid was not specifically covered by the DRA require-ements for Medicare, CMS issued guidance in July 2008 to help states appropriately align Medicaid inpatient hospital payment policies with Medicare's HAC payment policies.[30] CMS instructed state Medicaid agencies to implement policies to avoid payment liability when dual eligible (i.e., individuals eligible for both Medicare and Medicaid) beneficiaries had HACs. CMS also encouraged Medicaid agencies to implement policies to deny payment when other Medicaid beneficiaries developed complications during hospitalizations. CMS directed states to several Medicaid authorities to appropriately deny payment for HACs.

PPACA requires the Secretary to identify current state practices that prohibit payment for health care-acquired conditions and to incorporate into regulations these practices or elements of the practices that are applicable to Medicaid. The Secretary is required to issue regulations to prohibit federal Medicaid matching payments for health care-acquired conditions by July 1, 2011. These new regulations are to ensure that the prohibition on payments for health care-acquired conditions does not result in Medicaid beneficiaries losing access to services. PPACA requires the Secretary to define health care-acquired conditions consistent with Medicare's HAC definition, but may exclude certain conditions when they are inapplicable to Medicaid beneficiaries.

In implementing regulations governing Medicaid payment for health care acquired conditions, the Secretary is required to apply Medicare's regulations prohibiting hospital payments for HACs to the Medicaid program.

Prescription Drugs

Outpatient prescription drugs are an optional Medicaid benefit, but all states cover prescription drugs for most beneficiary groups. Medicaid law requires prescription drug manufacturers who wish to sell their products to Medicaid agencies to enter into rebate agreements with the Secretary on behalf of states. Under these agreements, drug manufacturers pay a rebate to state Medicaid agencies for drugs purchased for Medicaid beneficiaries, although purchases by Medicaid managed care organizations (MMCO) are exempted from the rebates.[31] In exchange for entering into rebate agreements, state Medicaid programs must cover all drugs (except certain statutorily excluded drug classes) marketed by those manufacturers. In 2004 CMS estimated that 550 pharmaceutical manufacturers participated in Medicaid's drug rebate program.[32]

For each prescription drug purchased by Medicaid, participating drug manufacturers must report two market prices to CMS—the average manufacturer price (AMP), which is the average price drug makers receive for sales to retail pharmacies and mail-order establishments, and the lowest transaction price, or best price, that manufacturers receive from sales to certain private buyers of each drug. Those prices, which serve as reference points for determining manufacturers' rebate obligations, must be reported for each formulation, dosage, and strength of prescription drugs purchased on behalf of Medicaid beneficiaries.

Prescription Drug Rebates

(P.L. 111-148: §2501)

For the purpose of determining rebates, Medicaid distinguishes between two types of drugs: (1) single source drugs (generally, those still under patent) and innovator multiple source drugs (drugs originally marketed under a patent or original new drug application but for which there now are generic equivalents); and (2) all other, non-innovator, multiple source drugs.

Rebates for the first category of drugs—drugs still under patent or those once covered by patents—have two components: a basic rebate and an additional rebate. Medicaid's basic rebate is determined by the larger of either a comparison of a drug's quarterly AMP to the best price for the same period, or a flat percentage (15.1%) of the drug's quarterly AMP. Drug manufacturers owe an additional rebate when their unit prices for individual products increase faster than inflation.

Under previous law, modifications to existing drugs—new dosages or formulations—generally are considered new products for purposes of reporting AMPs to CMS. As a result, drug makers sometimes can avoid incurring additional rebate obligations by making alterations to existing products, sometimes called line-extensions, and releasing these as new products. For example, manufacturers have developed new extended-release formulations of existing products which, because they are considered new products under existing Medicaid drug rebate rules, are given new base period AMPs. The new base period AMPs for line-extension products will be higher than the original product's AMP. For the line-extension product, the manufacturer is unlikely to owe an additional rebate since the product's AMP will not have risen faster than the rate of inflation.

Public Health Service Act (PHSA) Sec. 340B requires pharmaceutical drug manufacturers that enter into Medicaid drug rebate agreements to discount outpatient drugs purchased by certain public health facilities (covered entities). In addition to other requirements, 340B hospitals and other covered entities are prohibited from obtaining multiple discounts for individual drugs and from diverting 340B drug purchases to other buyers.

Beginning January 1, 2010, with certain exceptions, PPACA increases the flat rebate percentage used to calculate Medicaid's basic rebate for single source and innovator multiple source outpatient prescription drugs from 15.1% to 23.1% of AMP. The basic rebate percentage for multi-source, non-innovator and all other drugs increases from 11% to 13% of AMP.[33]

PPACA also requires the Secretary to recover the additional funds states received from drug manufacturers from increases in the basic Medicaid rebates. The Secretary is authorized to reduce Medicaid payments to states for the additional prescription drug rebates that resulted from increases in the minimum rebate percentages—the difference between 15.1% of AMP and 23.1% of AMP for single source products and the difference between 11% and 13% for generic products.

PPACA requires the Secretary to estimate the additional rebate amounts to recover from states based on utilization and other data. In addition, when it is determined that the recovered amount from a state for a previous quarter under-estimated the actual rebate amount (state share) the Secretary is required to make further adjustments to recover the additional rebates from states. These state payment reductions are considered overpayments to the state and disallowed against states' regular Medicaid quarterly draw, similar to other overpayments. These disallowances are not subject to reconsideration.

PPACA also requires drug manufacturers to pay rebates to states on drugs dispensed to Medicaid beneficiaries who receive care through Medicaid MCOs, similar to the way rebates are required under previous law for FFS beneficiaries. Medicaid capitation rates paid by states are to be adjusted to include these rebates, and Medicaid MCOs are subject to additional reporting requirements such as submitting data to states on the total number of units of each dose, strength, and package size by National Drug Code for each covered outpatient drug. Medicaid MCOs can utilize formularies as long as there is an exception process so that excluded drugs are available through a prior authorization process. Drugs discounted under 340B are excluded from the Medicaid rebate requirements under SSA Sec. 1927.

With certain exceptions, PPACA requires that additional rebates for new formulations of single source or innovator multiple source drugs be calculated as the greater of the basic rebate for new products or the AMP of the new drug multiplied by highest additional rebate for any strength of the original product (calculated for each dose and strength of the product).[34] However, total rebate liability for each dosage form and strength of an individual single source or innovator multiple source drug is capped at 100% of that drug's AMP. Other features of the drug rebate program, such Medicaid's best price requirement, are unchanged by PPACA. HCERA amended PPACA to clarify that the calculation of the additional rebate for new formulations of existing drugs (line extensions) applied to single source or innovator multiple source drugs only in oral solid dosage forms. Changes in this provision begin January 1, 2010, except for the MMCO rebates which begin March 23, 2010.

Elimination of Exclusion of Coverage of Certain Drugs

(P.L. 111-148: §2502)

Previous Medicaid law excludes coverage of 11 drug classes, including barbiturates, benzodiazepines, and smoking cessation products. States had the option to cover excluded drugs, and most states cover barbiturates, and benzodiazepines, and smoking cessation drugs. States received FFP when they cover these drugs. Coverage of prescription drugs for full benefit dual eligibles (individuals who are eligible for both Medicare and Medicaid) was transferred from state Medicaid programs to Medicare when Part D was implemented in January 2006. Barbiturates and benzodiazepines, two important drug classes for Medicaid beneficiaries, were excluded from Part D formularies (were not covered by Medicare Part D). However, under the Medicare Improvements for Patients and Providers Act of 2008 (MIPPA, P.L. 110-275), Medicare prescription drug plans and Medicare Advantage plans will be required to include benzodiazepines and barbiturates in their formularies for prescriptions dispensed beginning January 1, 2013.

PPACA requires that smoking cessation drugs, barbiturates, and benzodiazepines be removed from Medicaid's excluded drug list. When this provision takes effect beginning January 1, 2014, states that cover prescription drugs will be required to cover barbiturates, benzodiazepines, and smoking cessation products for most Medicaid beneficiaries.

Providing Adequate Pharmacy Reimbursement

(P.L. 111-148: §2503)

Medicaid law requires the Secretary to establish upper limits on payments to pharmacies for prescription drugs. These limits are intended to encourage substitution of lower-cost generic equivalents for more costly brand-name drugs. When applied to multiple source drugs, those limits are referred to as federal upper payment limits (FUL). CMS calculates FULs and periodically publishes these prices. DRA required the Secretary to use a new formula for FULs beginning January 1, 2007. The new FUL formula was to equal 250% of the average manufacturer price (AMP) of the least costly therapeutic equivalent. AMP was defined under DRA to be the average price paid to the manufacturer by wholesalers for drugs distributed to the retail pharmacy class of trade. DRA also reduced the number of multiple source products rated by the FDA as therapeutic and pharmaceutically equivalent from three to two. Manufacturers are required to report AMP to CMS. Previous law allows the Secretary to contract for a survey of retail prices that represent a nationwide average consumer drug price, net of all discounts and rebates.

National pharmacy associations challenged the legality of the DRA's FUL methodology published in a proposed rule CMS issued in 2007 because they claimed that for community pharmacies, the new FULs would be below drug acquisition costs. The court issued an injunction on December 19, 2007, which prohibited CMS from setting FULs for Medicaid covered generic drugs based on AMP, and from disclosing AMP data except within HHS or to the Department of Justice. The court's 2007 injunction was for an indefinite period and remains in place. In addition to the court injunction against using AMP to calculate Medicaid FULs, Section 203 of MIPPA imposed a moratorium on the use of AMP to set FULs and prohibited CMS from making AMP data available until October 1, 2009. MIPPA Section 203 authorized CMS to set FULs based on the pre-DRA methodology—150% of the lowest published price (i.e., wholesale acquisition cost, average wholesale price, or direct price) for each dosage and strength of generic drug products— until September 30, 2009. In general, these published prices are significantly higher than AMPs.

Under previous law, CMS lacked authority to use the pre-DRA formula (expired September 30, 2009) for setting FULs or the DRA authority (prohibited by MIPPA). In addition, CMS is bound by the court's injunction preventing the use of the DRA formula. On September 25, 2009, prior to the expiration of authority to use the pre-DRA formula, CMS issued a list of multiple source drug FULs to establish the federal maximum that states may pay under Medicaid. However, most states also use Medicaid Acquisition Costs (MACs) to set their own ceiling prices, and these prices often are less than FULs.

PPACA requires the Secretary to set FULs at 175% or more of the weighted average (determined on the basis of utilization) of the most recently reported monthly AMPs.[35] PPACA restores the pre-DRA definition of multiple source drugs as three therapeutic and pharmaceutically equivalent products. PPACA also includes technical changes to the FUL formula such as a smoothing process for average manufacturer prices to reduce short-term volatility and clarification that AMP excludes the following:

4. customary prompt pay discounts to wholesalers;
5. *bona fide* service fees paid by manufacturers to wholesalers and retail community pharmacies (RCPs), such as distribution service fees, inventory management fees, product stocking allowances, and administrative services agreements and patient care programs (medication compliance and patient education programs);
6. reimbursement by manufacturers for recalled, damaged, expired, or unsaleable returned goods;
7. payments received from, and rebates or discounts to, large purchasers such as pharmacy benefit managers, managed care organizations, health maintenance organizations, insurers, hospitals, clinics, mail order pharmacies, long-term care providers, manufacturers, or any other entity that does not conduct business as a wholesaler or a retail community pharmacy.

Further, PPACA revises the definition of a multiple source drug from one marketed in a state during the rebate period to a product marketed during the period in the United States. Moreover, PPACA expands drug pricing disclosure requirements to include monthly weighted average AMPs and retail survey prices. Manufacturers are required to report within 30 days of the end of each month of a rebate period the total number of units sold and used by the manufacturer to calculate the AMP for each covered outpatient drug. Assuming the court injunction is lifted, Section 2503 takes effect the first day of the first calendar quarter that begins at least six months after PPACA's enactment (January 1, 2011), regardless of whether final regulations were issued.

340B Prescription Drug Discount Program Expansion[36]

(P.L. 111-148: §7101-7103 as modified by P.L. 111-152: §2302)

Under Section 340B of the PHSA, pharmaceutical drug manufacturers that participate in the Medicaid drug rebate program are required to enter into pharmaceutical pricing agreements where they agree to discount covered outpatient drugs purchased by public health and related entities (covered entities). Covered entities include hospitals owned or operated by state or local governments that serve a high percentage of Medicaid beneficiaries, as well as federal grantees such as Federally Qualified Health Centers (FQHCs), FQHC look-alikes, family planning clinics, state-operated AIDS drug assistance programs, Ryan White CARE Act grantees, family planning and sexually transmitted disease clinics, and others, as identified in the PHSA. Covered entities do not receive discounts on inpatient drugs under the 340B program.

PPACA and HCERA expand the list of covered entities eligible to receive 340B discounts to include (1) certain children's and free-standing cancer hospitals excluded from the Medicare prospective payment system, (2) critical access and sole community hospitals, and (3) rural referral centers. PPACA requires the Secretary to develop systems to improve compliance and program integrity activities for manufacturers and covered entities, as well as administrative procedures to resolve disputes. Further, within 18 months of enactment (September 23, 2011), the Government Accountability Office (GAO) is required to submit to Congress a report that examines, among other issues, whether individuals receiving services through 340B covered entities receive optimal health care services. With the exception of the GAO report, the 340B changes are effective and apply to drug purchases that began January 1, 2010.[37]

Program Integrity

Program integrity (PI) initiatives are designed to combat fraud, waste, and abuse. This includes processes directed at reducing improper payments, as well as activities to prevent, detect, investigate, and ultimately prosecute health care fraud and abuse. More specifically, PI ensures that correct payments are made to legitimate providers for appropriate and reasonable services for eligible beneficiaries.

The federal government and states contribute equally to fund most Medicaid and CHIP activities to combat waste, fraud, and abuse, although for some activities, the federal government provides additional funds through enhanced matching rates. All states receive the same federal match rate for administrative expenditures, including most PI activities, which is generally 50%. States receive higher federal matching rates for selected administrative activities such as 90% for the design, development, and installation of required claims processing and information retrieval systems—Medicaid Management Information Systems (MMIS); 75% for the operation of approved MMIS; 90% for the start up of Medicaid Fraud Control Units (MFCUs); and 75% for ongoing MFCU operation.

Congress provided additional dedicated funding for Medicaid program integrity activities in the Deficit Reduction Act of 2005, (DRA, P.L. 109-171). Under DRA, among many other changes, Congress established a Medicaid Integrity Program (MIP) that included annual appropriations reaching $75 million. This MIP funding was to support and enhance state PI efforts by expanding and sustaining national PI activities in the areas of provider audits, overpayment identification, and payment integrity and quality of care education.

PPACA created additional requirements to increase uniformity, and bolster Medicare, Medicaid and CHIP PI activities. For instance, PPACA introduced additional provider screening requirements that are applicable to Medicare, Medicaid, and CHIP. PPACA creates an integrated Medicare and Medicaid data repository to enhance PI data sharing to be available to federal and state agencies and law enforcement officials. Moreover, PPACA established a recovery audit contractor (RAC) requirement for Medicaid (described below), similar to Medicare's RAC program.

Expansion of the Recovery Audit Contractor (RAC) Program

(P.L. 111-148: §6411)

RACs are private organizations that contract with CMS to identify and collect improper payments made in Medicare's FFS program. In the Medicare Prescription Drug, Improvement, and Modernization Act of 2003 (MMA, P.L. 108-173), Congress required the Secretary to conduct a three-year demonstration of RACs. In December 2006, Congress passed the Tax Relief and Health Care Act of 2006 (TRHCA, P.L. 109-43 2) which made the RAC program permanent and mandated its expansion nationwide by January 1, 2010. The TRHCA RAC expansion still applied only to Medicare Parts A and B, excluding managed care under Medicare Part C and prescription drug coverage under Part D. CMS began the national rollout of the permanent RAC program in 19 states in March 2009.

PPACA requires states to establish by December 31, 2010, contracts, consistent with state law and similar to the contracts the Secretary has established for the Medicare RAC program, with one or more RACs. These state RACs are to identify underpayments, overpayments, and recoup overpayments made for services provided under state Medicaid plans as well as waivers. The state Medicaid RAC program is subject to exceptions and requirements the Secretary may establish. In addition, states are required to make certain assurances for their RAC programs, including that the RAC (1) operates on a contingency basis; (2) has an appeal process for adverse determinations in place; (3) recoveries are subject to quarterly expenditure estimates; and (4) coordinate with other PI organizations such as federal and state law enforcement agencies.

Termination of Provider Participation under Medicaid if Terminated under Medicare or Other State Health Care Program

(P.L. 111-148: §6501)

Under previous Medicaid law, subject to certain exceptions, the Secretary is required to exclude providers or individuals from Medicare or Medicaid that (1) have been convicted of a criminal offense related to the delivery of an item or service under Medicare or under any state health care program; (2) have been convicted, under federal or state law, of a criminal offense relating to neglect or abuse of patients in connection with the delivery of a health care item or service; (3) have been convicted of a felony related to health care fraud, theft, embezzlement, breach of fiduciary responsibility, or other financial misconduct; or (4) have been convicted of a felony relating to the unlawful manufacture, distribution, prescription, or dispensing of a controlled substance.

The Secretary also may exclude providers or individuals from Medicare or Medicaid participation who are involved in prohibited activities, such as program-related convictions, license revocation, failure to supply information, and default on loan or scholarship obligations. CMS is required to promptly notify the Department of Health and Human Services Office of the Inspector General (HHS/OIG) if it receives Medicare or Medicaid program participation applications that identify providers who have engaged in prohibited activities.

PPACA requires states to terminate individuals or entities (or individuals or entities who owned, controlled, or managed entities) from their Medicaid programs if the entities have unpaid Medicaid overpayments (as defined by the Secretary), were suspended, excluded or terminated from Medicaid or Medicare participation, or were affiliated with individuals or entities who had been terminated from Medicaid. The changes in this provision are effective January 1, 2011.

Medicaid Exclusion from Participation Relating to Certain Ownership, Control, and Management Affiliations

(P.L. 111-148: §6502)

Previous Medicaid law requires states to exclude individuals or entities from Medicaid participation when states are directed to do so by the Secretary, and to deny payment for any item or service furnished by the individual or entity. States are required to exclude these individuals and deny payment for a period specified by the Secretary.

PPACA requires Medicaid agencies to exclude individuals or entities from Medicaid participation if the entity or individual owns, controls, or manages an entity that (1) has unpaid or unreturned overpayments during the period as determined by the Secretary or the state; (2) is suspended, excluded, or terminated from participation in any Medicaid program; or (3) is affiliated with an individual or entity that has been suspended, excluded, or terminated from Medicaid participation during the period. This provision is effective January 1, 2011 (see §6508, General Effective Date below).

Billing Agents, Clearinghouses, or Other Alternate Payees Required to Register under Medicaid

(P.L. 111-148: §6503)

As a condition of participation, certification, or recertification in Medicaid, the Secretary requires disclosing entities to supply upon request, either to the Secretary or the state Medicaid agency, information on the identity of each person with ownership or control interests in the entity or subcontractor that is equal to 5% or more of such entity. Disclosing entities include providers of service, independent clinical laboratories, renal disease facilities, managed care organizations or health maintenance organizations, entities (other than individual practitioners or groups of practitioners) that furnish or arrange for services, carriers or other agencies, or organizations that act as fiscal intermediaries or agents for service providers. Federal rules applicable to Medicaid state plans also require states to exclude individuals or entities from Medicaid participation when a state is directed to do so by the Secretary and to deny payment for any item or service furnished by the individual or entity.

This provision in PPACA requires any agents, clearinghouses, or other alternate payees that submit claims on behalf of Medicaid health care providers to register with the state and the Secretary in a form and manner the Secretary is required to specify. This provision is effective January 1, 2011 (see §6508, General Effective Date below).

Requirement to Report Expanded Set of Data Elements under MMIS to Detect Fraud and Abuse

(P.L. 111-148: §6504)

To administer their state Medicaid plans, states are required to operate an automated claims processing system and database known as a Medicaid Management Information System (MMIS). The Secretary approves states' MMISs and determines if they have met requirements including compatibility with Medicare claims processing and information systems and consistency with uniform coding systems for claims processing and data interchange. MMISs also are required to be capable of providing timely and accurate data, meet other specifications as required by the Secretary, and provide for electronic transmission of claims data as well as be consistent with Medicaid Statistical Information Systems (MSIS) data formats. MSIS is an analytical database derived from MMIS claims level data. MMIS data primarily captures claims data when Medicaid beneficiaries receive their care on a FFS basis. For most states, managed care encounter data or managed care claims level data generally are not reported or otherwise captured by state MMIS systems. Medicaid managed care organizations (MMCO) are paid a capitated (fixed fee) regardless of the amount of care required by beneficiaries. Encounter data reporting requirements under state contracts with MMCOs vary. Medicaid agencies also do not report claims level managed care data to CMS through their MMISs.

Beginning in January 1, 2011, PPACA requires states to collect and submit through their MMISs managed care data as identified by the Secretary for program integrity, program oversight, and administration. The Secretary is to determine the data needed and how frequently these data are required to be submitted. In addition, for contract years beginning after January 1, 2010, MMCOs are required to submit data elements as determined necessary by the Secretary for program integrity, program oversight, and administration.

Prohibition on Payments to Institutions or Entities Located Outside of the United States

(P.L. 111-148: §6505)

Under previous Medicaid law, there were no specific prohibitions or limitations which prevent Medicaid payments to institutions or entities located outside the United States. This provision in PPACA prohibits states from making any payments for items or services supplied to beneficiaries under a Medicaid state plan or waiver to any financial institution or entity located outside of the United States. This Section is effective January 1, 2011 (see §6508, General Effective Date below).

Overpayments

(P.L. 111-148: §6506)

Previous Medicaid law requires states to repay promptly the federal share of Medicaid overpayments when the state discovers overpayments occurred. States had 60 days after discovery of an overpayment to recover, or attempt to recover, the overpayment before an adjustment was made to their federal matching payment. Adjustments in federal payments were made at the end of the 60 days, whether or not states had recovered the funds. When states were unable to recover overpayments because the debts were discharged in bankruptcy or were otherwise uncollectable, an exception to the 60-day rule was provided and federal matching payments were not adjusted.

Beginning with enactment, PPACA extends the time period for states to repay overpayments due to fraud to one year when a determination of the amount of the overpayment was not made due to an ongoing judicial or administrative process, including the appeal of a judgment. When these overpayments due to fraud are pending, state repayments of the federal portion are not due until 30 days after the date of the final judgment (including a final appeal determination). PPACA requires the Secretary to issue regulations for states to use in adapting MMIS edits, conducting audits, or other appropriate actions to identify and correct recurring or ongoing overpayments. This provision went into effect March 23, 2010.

Mandatory State Use of National Correct Coding Initiative

(P.L. 111-148: §6507)

Working through health insurance contractors, CMS processes Part B Medicare claims which include payments for physician, laboratory, and radiology services. In 1996, to help ensure correct payment for these claims, CMS initiated a national correct coding initiative (NCCI). Under NCCI, CMS's contractors screen Medicare Part B claims with automated pre-payment edits. The software edits used by Medicare contractors are designed to detect anomalies that indicate a claim has incorrect information. For example, NCCI edits can detect claims with duplicate services delivered to the same beneficiary on the same date of service. Medicaid law does not require the use of NCCI prepayment edits, but individual states conduct medical review and other pre- and post-payment reviews designed to detect fraud, waste, and abuse.

Beginning with claims submitted on October 1, 2010, PPACA requires states to add to their MMISs pre-payment edits to correct and control improper coding, similar to the NCCI edits used by Medicare contractors. By September 1, 2010, the Secretary is required to (1) identify NCCI methodologies compatible with Medicaid claims, and (2) identify methodologies applicable to Medicaid, but for which no Medicare NCCI methodologies had been established. Further, the Secretary is required to notify states of NCCI methodologies (or successor initiatives) applicable to Medicaid that were identified and how states are to incorporate those methodologies into their Medicaid claims processing systems. Moreover, the Secretary is required to submit a report to Congress by March 1, 2011, that includes the notice to states about the NCCI methodologies, and an analysis that supports the identification of NCCI methodologies to be applied to Medicaid claims.

General Effective Date for Medicaid and CHIP Program Integrity Activities

(P.L. 111-148: §6508)

States are required to implement PPACA's Medicaid program integrity Sections by January 1, 2011, regardless of whether final regulations were issued. In situations where the Secretary determined that state legislation would be required (other than appropriation legislation) to amend the state plan or child health plan, then states will have additional time to comply with these requirements.

Other Program Integrity and Related Provisions Applicable to Medicaid

Provider Screening and Other Enrollment Requirements under Medicare, Medicaid, and CHIP

(P.L. 111-148: §6401 as amended by §10603)

The process for enrolling providers and suppliers in Medicare, Medicaid, and CHIP is different depending on the program and the type of provider, although Medicaid and CHIP requirements are similar. PPACA requires the Secretary, in consultation with the HHS/OIG, to establish similar procedures for screening providers and suppliers enrolling in the Medicare, Medicaid, and CHIP programs. These procedures are required to include processes for screening providers, enhanced oversight measures, disclosure requirements, moratoriums on enrollment, and requirements for developing compliance programs.

By January 1, 2011, the Secretary is required to develop procedures, which apply to both new and current providers. The Secretary is required to implement these requirements within three years. Further, the Secretary is required to determine the level of screening for providers depending on the provider's fraud risk category (as determined by the Secretary). At a minimum, all providers and suppliers are subject to licensure checks, including checks across states.

The Secretary has authority to impose additional screening requirements such as criminal background checks, fingerprinting, unannounced site visits, database checks, and periods of enhanced oversight if necessary. To cover the costs of the screening, new institutional providers and suppliers are subject to application fees, with some hardship exceptions and waivers for certain Medicaid providers when states can demonstrate that imposition of the fees might jeopardize beneficiaries' access to services. Fees start at $500 for institutional providers and are adjusted for inflation thereafter; individual providers are exempt from application fees. The Secretary also has authority to impose a temporary moratorium on enrolling new providers if necessary. Further, PPACA requires Medicare, Medicaid, and CHIP providers and suppliers, within a particular industry or category, to establish compliance programs that adhere to standards established by the Secretary and the HHS/OIG.

Enhanced Medicare and Medicaid Program Integrity Provisions

(P.L. 111-148: §6402, as modified by P.L. 111-152: §1304)

PPACA requires the Secretary to enhance existing Medicare, Medicaid, and CHIP program integrity initiatives. As part of these enhancements, the Secretary is required to apply some of the same requirements to Medicare, Medicaid, and CHIP.

- ***Data Matching.*** Under previous law, claims and payment data for Medicare and Medicaid are housed in multiple databases. CMS is in the process of consolidating information stored in these databases into an Integrated Data Repository (IDR). This provision in PPACA requires CMS to include in the IDR claims and payment data from the following programs: Medicare (Parts A, B, C, and D), Medicaid, CHIP, health-related programs administered by the Departments of Veterans Affairs (VA) and Defense (DOD), Social Security Administration, and the Indian Health Service (IHS). The priority is to be given to integration of Medicare and Medicaid claims and payment data. Other program data, including CHIP, will be integrated as appropriate.
- ***Access to Data.*** Inspectors General have substantial independence and power to carry out their mandate to combat waste, fraud, and abuse, including relatively unlimited authority to access all records and information of an agency. This provision in PPACA grants the

HHS/OIG and the DOJ explicit access to Medicare, Medicaid, and CHIP payment and claims data (including Medicare Part D data) to conduct law enforcement and oversight activities. This provision further grants the HHS/OIG the authority to obtain information from providers, suppliers, beneficiaries (as long as privacy protections are observed) including supporting documentation necessary to validate payment claims, such as medical records, but also any records necessary for evaluation of the economy, efficiency, and effectiveness of Medicare and Medicaid programs.

- ***Beneficiary Participation in Health Care Fraud Scheme.*** This provision in PPACA requires the Secretary to impose administrative penalties on beneficiaries entitled to or enrolled in Medicare, Medicaid, or CHIP if they knowingly participate in health care fraud offenses. In addition, beneficiaries are required to return overpayments within 60 days of receipt of those payments or be subject to enforcement action.
- ***National Provider Identifier (NPI).*** Health care providers often have multiple provider numbers, one number for billing each private insurance plan or public health care program. The administrative simplification provisions of Health Insurance Portability and Accountability Act of 1996 (HIPAA, P.L. 104-191) required the adoption and use of a standard unique identifier for health care providers or NPI. All health care providers who are considered covered entities under HIPAA were required to obtain and submit claims using an NPI as of May 2007. This provision requires the Secretary to issue regulations before January 1, 2011, mandating that all Medicare and Medicaid providers include NPIs on all payment claims and enrollment applications.
- ***Withholding of Federal Matching Payments for States that Fail to Report Enrollee Encounter Data in the Medicaid Statistical Information System (MSIS).*** The Secretary is permitted to withhold federal matching payments for services provided to Medicaid beneficiaries if states do not report encounter data to MSIS (as determined by the Secretary) for those beneficiaries in timely manner (as determined by the Secretary).
- ***Permissive Exclusions.*** HHS/OIG has the authority to exclude health care providers from federal health care program participation. Exclusions are mandatory in some circumstances, and permissive in others (i.e., HHS/OIG has discretion in whether to exclude an entity

or individual). This provision subjects individuals or entities that make false statements or misrepresentations on applications to enroll or participate in federal health care programs to the OIG's permissive exclusion authority. The provision explicitly applies to Medicare Advantage plans, Prescription Drug Plans, and MMCOs as well as these entities' participating providers and suppliers.

- ***Civil Monetary Penalties (CMPs).*** Previous law authorized the imposition of CMPs on individuals, organizations, agencies, or other entities that engage in improper conduct under federal health care programs. PPACA provides for CMPs of up to $10,000 for each false claim submitted, $15,000 or $50,000 under other circumstances, and an assessment of up to three times the amount claimed. PPACA also adds additional actions that are subject to CMPs. Among other changes, the following individuals are subject to CMPs: those who have been excluded from a federal health care program, but who order or prescribe an item or service; those who make false statements on enrollment applications, bids, or contracts; and those who know of an overpayment and do not return the overpayment.
- ***Testimonial Subpoena Authority***. Under PPACA, the Secretary has authority to issue subpoenas and require the attendance and testimony of witnesses and the production of any other evidence that relates to matters under investigation or in question by the Secretary. The Secretary also can delegate this authority to the HHS/OIG and the CMS administrator for program exclusion investigations.
- ***Increased Medicare and Medicaid Integrity Program Funding***. Under the Medicare Integrity Program, CMS contracts with private entities to conduct a variety of activities designed to protect Medicare from fraud, waste, and abuse. Activities include auditing providers, identifying and recovering improper payments, educating providers about fraudulent providers, and instituting a Medicare-Medicaid data matching program.

DRA established a comparable program for Medicaid, the Medicaid Integrity Program (MIP). The Medicaid MIP provides dedicated resources to contract with entities to reduce fraud, waste, and abuse. PPACA requires both Medicare and Medicaid Integrity Program contractors to supply the Secretary and the HHS/OIG with performance statistics, including the number and amount of overpayments recovered, the number of fraud referrals, and the return on investment for these activities. The Secretary also is required to conduct evaluations of eligible entities at least every three years. Within six months of each fiscal year end, the Secretary is required to submit a report to Congress that describes the use and effectiveness of MIP funds.

Section 6402 of PPACA increased Health Care Fraud and Abuse Control (HCFAC) account funding. HCFAC funds are used for a number of health care fraud and abuse activities, but the majority of the funds are used for Medicare activities. HCERA (Sec. 1304) further increases those HCFAC funds, bringing them up to the levels proposed in the House health care reform bill, the Affordable Health Care for America Act (H.R. 3962). In addition, HCERA amended PPACA and increased MIP funding by indexing MIP funds to annual changes in the consumer price index, beginning with FY2010.

Improving Nursing Home Transparency, Enforcement, and Staff Training

(P.L. 111-148: §6101-§6107, §6111-§6114, and §6121)

Previous Medicare and Medicaid law requires skilled nursing facilities (SNF) and nursing facilities (NF) to be administered in a manner that will ensure residents' well-being. The Secretary was required to establish SNF and NF requirements to protect the safety, health, welfare, and rights of residents. Facilities undergo regular survey and certification inspections to ensure their compliance with these standards. SNF and NF inspections identify deficiencies where facilities fail to meet federal standards. Deficiencies can range from minor problems to major safety and life-threatening conditions. State and federal officials may impose civil monetary penalties on facilities that fail to meet standards or fail to correct deficiencies. In extreme cases, federal and state officials can install new facility management, assume control of facilities, or even close SNF or NFs that jeopardize residents' well-being.

PPACA enhances certain accountability requirements for Medicare certified SNFs and Medicaid certified NFs. The changes in these sections require SNFs and NFs to maintain and make available additional information on facility ownership and organizational structure, as well as to establish new staff compliance and ethics training programs. Further, these sections require the Secretary to establish additional requirements for SNFs and NFs to develop and implement compliance and ethics programs.

The Secretary is required to enhance the SNF and NF information available on the Medicare Nursing Home Compare website, and to ensure that information is prominent, easily accessible, searchable, and readily understandable to long-term care (LTC) consumers. SNFs are required to report wage and benefit expenditures for direct care staff. In addition, the Secretary, in consultation with private sector experts, is required to redesign Medicare and Medicaid cost reports to capture wage and benefit reporting by SNFs and NFs. The Secretary is required to develop a new standardized complaint form that facilities and states are required to make available to all stakeholders and consumers. The changes in these sections require SNFs and NFs to electronically report direct staffing information to the Secretary following specifications the Secretary establishes in consultation with stakeholders. GAO is required to conduct a study of CMS's nursing home Five-Star rating system. PPACA establishes additional civil money penalties that both the Secretary and states have authority to impose on SNFs or NFs found to have quality of care issues and other deficiencies that jeopardized residents' safety. The Secretary is required to develop, test, and implement a national independent monitoring demonstration for large interstate and intrastate SNF and NF chains.

Further, PPACA establishes new requirements for SNF and NF administrators to inform residents and their representatives, as well as the Secretary, states, and other stakeholders of planned facility closures. SNF and NF administrators who fail to comply with the closure notice requirements are subject to penalties up to $100,000 and exclusion from federal health program participation. The Secretary also is required to conduct demonstration projects on best practices for culture change and use of information technology in SNFs and NFs. Moreover, PPACA requires the Secretary to revise initial nurse aide training, competency, and evaluation requirements to include dementia and abuse prevention. Finally, PPACA authorizes the Secretary to revise dementia management training and patient abuse prevention in ongoing nurse training, competency, and evaluation requirements.

Demonstrations and Grant Funding

Money Follows the Person

(P.L. 111-148: §2403)

Under the Money Follows the Person (MFP) Rebalancing Demonstration, the Secretary awarded competitive grants to states to meet the following objectives: (1) increase the use of home and community-based, rather than institutional, long-term care (LTC) services; (2) eliminate barriers that prevent or restrict the flexible use of Medicaid funds to support services for individuals in settings of their choice; (3) increase Medicaid's ability to assure home and community-based LTC services to individuals transitioning from institutions to a community settings; and (4) ensure that procedures are in place to provide quality assurance home and community-based LTC services. To participate, individuals must be (1) residing in, and have been residing in for not less than six months and not more than two years, an inpatient facility; (2) receiving Medicaid benefits for inpatient services furnished by such inpatient facility; and (3) continuing to require the level of care provided in an inpatient facility, among other requirements.

P.L. 111-148 extends the MFP Rebalancing Demonstration through September 30, 2016, and extends the deadline for the submission of the final evaluation report to September 30, 2016. The provision also changes the demonstration's eligibility rules by requiring that individuals reside in an inpatient facility for not less than 90 consecutive days, and by removing the maximum length of stay for eligibility purposes. The provision excludes Medicare-covered short-term rehabilitative services from counting toward the 90-day period. This provision become effective 30 days after enactment.

Demonstration Project to Evaluate Integrated Care around Hospitalization

(P.L. 111-148: §2704)

There is no related provision in prior law. The law establishes a Medicaid demonstration that will evaluate whether quality can be improved and Medicare payments reduced by making bundled payments to hospitals and physicians for the delivery of integrated care. Such payments will be made for episodes of care that include beneficiaries' hospital stays and concurrent physician services. Under the demonstration, bundled payments will be based on the beneficiary's severity of illness, among other requirements. States can target selected categories of beneficiaries, such as those with particular diagnoses, or those in particular geographic regions. Finally, participating hospitals will be required to have, or to establish, robust discharge planning programs that appropriately place beneficiaries in, or ensure that they have access to, post-acute care settings. This demonstration project is limited to eight states, and is required to begin on January 1, 2012, and end on December 31, 2016.

Medicaid Global Payment System Demonstration Project

(P.L. 111-148: §2705)

Under Medicaid fee-for-service, the state directly (or through a fiscal intermediary) pays for each covered service received by a Medicaid beneficiary. All states pay Medicaid-certified hospitals using a prospectively determined payment system for each case or day of hospitalization. Aggregate Medicaid payments vary based on the number of cases.

Under P.L. 111-148, the Secretary, in coordination with the Center for Medicare and Medicaid Innovation is required to establish the Medicaid Global Payment System Demonstration Project in no more than five states. The demonstration is required to be operational from FY20 10 through FY2012. Under the project, payments to an eligible safety net[38] hospital system or network will be adjusted from a FFS payment structure to a global, capitated payment model (a fixed-dollar payment for patient care, which does not vary by the amount of services delivered). The Secretary will have the authority to modify or terminate the project during an initial testing period, and will be required to submit an evaluation by the Innovation Center, as well as recommendations for legislative and administrative action, no later than 12 months after the demonstration's completion. The law authorizes to be appropriated such sums as necessary to finance this demonstration project.

Pediatric Accountable Care Organization Demonstration Project

(P.L. 111-148: §2706)

Accountable care organizations (ACOs) are defined by experts as groups of providers (e.g., combinations of one or more hospitals, physician groups, and/or other health care providers) that are jointly responsible, through shared bonuses or penalties, for the quality and cost of health care services for a given population of beneficiaries. Under the Medicare Shared Savings Program established under P.L. 111-148, groups of providers who voluntarily meet certain statutory criteria, including quality measurements, will be recognized as ACOs and be eligible to share in the cost-savings they achieve for the Medicare program. Under the new program, an eligible ACO is defined as a group of providers and suppliers who have an established mechanism for joint decision-making, and participate in the shared savings program for a minimum of three years, among other requirements. An ACO will include practitioners (physicians—regardless of specialty, nurse practitioners, physician assistants, and clinical nurse specialists) in group practice arrangements; networks of practices; and partnerships or joint-venture arrangements between hospitals and practitioners, among others.

The health reform law also establishes the Pediatric Accountable Care Organization demonstration project, where participating states are authorized to allow pediatric medical providers who voluntarily meet certain statutory criteria, including quality measurement criteria, to be recognized as ACOs. Such ACOs are also authorized to share in the cost savings they achieve for the Medicaid program, in the same manner as an ACO is recognized and provided with incentive payments under the newly established Medicare Shared Savings Program. ACOs can include pediatric physicians in group practice arrangements, or in networks of practices, and those in joint-venture arrangements with hospitals, among others. To receive an incentive payment, qualified ACOs will be required to meet both quality performance guidelines created by the Secretary, in consultation with states and pediatric providers, and a minimum annual savings level, as established by a participating state, for expenditures on items and services covered under Medicaid and CHIP. The Secretary is responsible for determining the amount of the annual incentive payment, which will be a portion of savings and can establish an annual cap on total incentive payments. The law authorizes an appropriation of such sums as may be necessary to finance this demonstration project.

Medicaid Emergency Psychiatric Demonstration Project

(P.L. 111-148: §2707)

Medicaid does not reimburse for services provided to residents of institutions for mental disease (IMD), except to those individuals who are under age 21 receiving inpatient psychiatric care and to individuals age 65 and over. IMDs are defined under Medicaid statute as hospitals, nursing facilities, or other institutions with more than 16 beds that are primarily engaged in providing diagnosis and treatment of persons with mental diseases.

Federal law requires that hospital-based IMDs which have emergency departments provide a medical screening examination to individuals for whom an examination or treatment for a medical condition is requested. In such cases, the hospital-based IMD must provide for an appropriate medical screening examination to determine whether or not a medical emergency exists. If a medical emergency exists, then the hospital-based IMD must provide, within the staff and facilities available at the hospital, for further medical examination and treatment as may be required to stabilize the medical condition, or to transfer the individual to another medical facility, subject to certain limitations.

The new law establishes a three-year Medicaid demonstration project in which eligible states are required to reimburse certain IMDs that are not publicly owned or operated for services provided to Medicaid eligibles, aged 21 through 64, who require medical assistance to stabilize a psychiatric emergency medical condition, as defined by the provision. A participating state is required to establish a mechanism for in-stay review (to be applied before the third day of the inpatient stay) to determine whether the patient has been stabilized, as defined by the provision. Eligible states will be selected by the Secretary based on geographic diversity. Out of funds not otherwise appropriated, the provision provides budget authority in advance of appropriations in an amount equal to $75 million for FY2011. Such funds will remain available for obligation for five years through December 31, 2015.

The Secretary is required to conduct an evaluation to determine the impact of this demonstration project. The evaluation will include an assessment of access to inpatient mental health services, average lengths of stays, emergency room utilization, discharge planning, impact on other mental health service costs, and a recommendation regarding whether the project should be continued beyond December 31, 2013, and expanded on a national basis. The Secretary is required to submit a final report to Congress no later than December 31, 2013.

Grants for School-Based Health Centers

(P.L. 111-148: §4101(a))

P.L. 111-148 creates a grant program to support the establishment of school-based health centers. This new law appropriates $50 million for each fiscal year from FY2010 through FY2013, for a total of $200 million, to remain available until expended. The use of such funds is prohibited for any service that is not authorized or allowed by federal, state, or local law. The Secretary is required to establish criteria and application procedures for awarding grants under this program. The Secretary will give preference in awarding grants to school-based health centers serving a large population of children eligible for Medicaid or CHIP. Eligible entities must use these grant funds only for expenditures for facilities, equipment or similar costs. No grant funds can be used for personnel or health care expenditures. (Another provision, described in a separate CRS report,[39] provides grants under the Public Health Service Act for the *operation* of school-based health centers.)

Incentives for Prevention of Chronic Diseases in Medicaid

(P.L. 111-148: §4108)

The Secretary is authorized to award grants to states to provide incentives for Medicaid beneficiaries to participate in programs to promote healthy lifestyles. These programs must be comprehensive and uniquely suited to address the needs of Medicaid eligible beneficiaries, and have demonstrated success in helping individuals lower cholesterol and/or blood pressure, lose or control weight, quit smoking and/or manage or prevent diabetes, and may address co-morbidities, such as depression, associated with these conditions. The purpose of this initiative is to test approaches that may encourage behavior modification and determine scalable solutions.

The provision appropriates $100 million in funding for these grants during a five-year period. Under the new law, the Secretary is required to award grants beginning on January 1, 2011, or the date on which the Secretary develops program criteria, whichever is earlier. These criteria are to be developed using relevant evidence-based research including the Guide to Community Preventive Services, the Guide to Clinical Preventive Services, and the National Registry of Evidence-Based Programs and Practices. The state initiatives must last at least three years of the five-year program spanning January 1, 2011, through January 1, 2016.

After the Secretary develops and institutes an outreach and education campaign to make states aware of the grants, states may submit a proposal and apply for funds to provide incentives to Medicaid enrollees who successfully complete healthy lifestyle programs. States are permitted to collaborate with community-based programs, non-profit organizations, providers, and faith-based groups, among others. States awarded such grants will be required to conduct an outreach and education campaign aimed at Medicaid beneficiaries and providers. They will also be required to establish a system to track beneficiary participation and validate changes in health risk and outcomes; establish standards and health status targets for participating Medicaid beneficiaries; evaluate the effectiveness of the program and provide the Secretary these evaluations; report to the Secretary on processes that have been developed and lessons learned; and report on preventive services as part of reporting on quality measures of Medicaid managed care programs. A state that is awarded a grant will be required to submit semi-annual reports, including information on the specific use of the funds, an assessment of program implementation, quality improvements and clinical outcomes, and an estimate of cost savings resulting from the program. This provision exempts states from the requirement 1902(a)(1) of the SSA, which relates to the statewide accessibility for medical assistance programs.

The Secretary is required to enter into a contract with an independent entity or organization to conduct an evaluation of the initiatives. This report should address the effect of the state initiative on the utilization of health care services, the extent to which special populations, such as adults with disabilities, are able to participate in the program, the level of satisfaction experienced by the Medicaid beneficiaries, and the additional administrative costs incurred as a result of providing the incentives.

The Secretary is required to submit an initial report to Congress before January 1, 2014. This initial report should include an interim evaluation based on information provided by states and recommendations on whether funding for expanding or extending the initiatives should continue beyond January 1, 2016. The Secretary is then required to submit a final report before July 1, 2016, that will include the independent contractor assessment together with recommendations for appropriate legislative and administrative actions.

Any incentives received by a beneficiary will not be considered for the purpose of determining eligibility for, or benefits under, any program funded whole or in part with federal funds, such as Medicaid.

Funding of Childhood Obesity Demonstration Project

(P.L. 111-148: §4306)

CHIPRA included several provisions designed to improve the quality of care under Medicaid and CHIP. Among other quality initiatives, this law directed the Secretary of HHS to initiate a demonstration to develop a comprehensive and systematic model for reducing child obesity. A total of $25 million was authorized to be appropriated over FY2009 through FY2013. P.L. 111- 148 replaces the authorization in current law with an appropriation of $25 million for fiscal years 2010 through 2014, to carry out the comprehensive demonstration project for reducing childhood obesity.

State Children's Health Insurance Program (CHIP)

CHIP provides health care coverage to low-income, uninsured children in families with income above Medicaid income standards. States may also extend CHIP coverage to pregnant women when certain conditions are met. In designing their CHIP programs, states may choose to expand Medicaid, create a stand-alone program, or use a combined approach. Federal CHIP appropriations are currently provided through FY2013.

Like Medicaid, CHIP is a joint federal-state program. For each dollar of state spending, the federal government makes a matching payment drawn from CHIP allotments. A state's share of program spending for Medicaid is the percentage *not* paid by the federal government through the FMAP. But for CHIP, the federal share is higher. That is, the enhanced FMAP (E-FMAP) for CHIP lowers the state's share of CHIP expenditures by 30% compared to the regular Medicaid FMAP. Although uncommon, certain types of CHIP expenditures are reimbursed at a rate different than the E-FMAP, and certain types of Medicaid expenditures are reimbursed at the EFMAP rate. For FY2010, the E-FMAP for CHIP ranges from 65% to 83%.

Beneficiary cost-sharing varies depending upon how a state designs its CHIP program. For CHIP Medicaid expansions, nominal amounts may apply as specified under the Medicaid program. For CHIP stand-alone programs, higher amounts may apply based on income level. In both cases, preventive services are exempt from all cost-sharing, and aggregate cost-sharing for all individuals is capped at 5% of family income.

P.L. 111-148 makes a number of changes to CHIP for future years. These changes are described below. (Other provisions affecting both Medicaid and CHIP are described in other sections of this report.)

Additional Federal Financing Participation for CHIP

(P.L. 111-148: §2101 as modified by §10203(c); P.L. 111-152: §1004(b)(2))

P.L. 111-148 maintains the current CHIP structure, and provides CHIP appropriations through FY2015. In the event that future federal CHIP allotments are insufficient to provide coverage to all eligible CHIP children, states will be required to establish procedures to ensure that such children not eligible for Medicaid receive coverage through certified plans in state-established exchanges.

Under P.L. 111-148, states will receive a 23 percentage point increase in the CHIP match rate (EFMAP), subject to a cap of 100%, for FY2016 through FY20 19 (although no CHIP appropriations are provided for those years). The 23 percentage point increase will not apply to certain expenditures.[40]

Upon enactment, states will be required to maintain income eligibility levels for CHIP through September 30, 2019, as a condition of receiving payments under Medicaid (notwithstanding the lack of corresponding federal appropriations for FY20 16 through FY20 19). Specifically, with the exception of waiting lists for enrolling children in CHIP or enrolling CHIP-eligible children in certified exchange plans when federal CHIP funding is no longer available, states can *not* implement eligibility standards, methodologies, or procedures that are *more* restrictive than those in place on the date of enactment. However, states can expand their current income eligibility levels—that is, states can enact *less* restrictive standards, methodologies or procedures.

In the event that federal CHIP allotments are not available after September 30, 2015, the only exchange plans available to children who would have been eligible for CHIP will be those that have been certified by the Secretary. With respect to such certification, not later than April 1, 2015, for each state, the Secretary will be required to review the benefits offered for children and the associated cost-sharing for exchange plans, and must certify that such plans have been determined to be at least comparable to the benefits and cost-sharing protections provided under each state's CHIP plan. States will be required to establish procedures to ensure that such children are screened for eligibility for Medicaid (under the state plan or a state waiver), and if found eligible, enrolled in Medicaid. In the case of children who, as a result of such screening, are determined to not be eligible for Medicaid, the state will be required to establish procedures to ensure that those children are enrolled in a certified exchange plan.

Prior to PPACA, for FY2009 through FY2013, states can receive bonus payments when their Medicaid enrollment among children exceeds a defined baseline, and they also implement certain outreach and enrollment activities. Under P.L. 111-148, the Medicaid enrollment bonuses included in CHIPRA (P.L. 111-3) will not apply beyond the current authorization period; bonus payments will not be available after FY2013.

Beginning January 1, 2014, states will be required to use modified adjusted gross income (MAGI) to determine Medicaid and CHIP eligibility (excluding Express Lane determinations), premiums and cost-sharing. States will be required to treat as CHIP children those who are determined to be ineligible for Medicaid due to the new provision eliminating income disregards based on expense or type of income. In addition, the CHIP benefit package and cost-sharing rules will continue as under current law.

Finally, a new Medicaid section added by P.L. 111-148 regarding Medicaid programs' coordination with state health insurance exchanges will also apply to CHIP programs.

Distribution of CHIP Allotments among States

(P.L. 111-148: §2101 as modified by §10203(d))

Prior to PPACA, federal CHIP allotments were appropriated through FY2013, with an allotment formula that was similar for all recent odd-numbered years and for all recent even-numbered years. PPACA extends federal CHIP allotments by two years and makes the allotments for FY2014 and FY2015 similar to how they were to occur in FY2012 and FY2013 under prior law.

In particular, based on prior law, for FY2012, the allotment for a state (or territory) will be calculated as the prior-year allotment and any prior-year Contingency Fund spending (for states that experience shortfalls of federal CHIP funds; described in further detail below), multiplied by the state's growth factor for the year.[41] Under PPACA, this will also be the basis for states' FY2014 allotments.

Based on prior law for FY2013, the allotment for a state (or territory) will be "rebased," based on prior year spending. This will be done by multiplying the state's growth factor for the year by the new base, which will be the prior year's federal CHIP spending. Under PPACA, this will also be the basis for states' FY2015 allotments.

As per prior law, the Child Enrollment Contingency Fund (created under CHIPRA) was established to prevent states from experiencing shortfalls of federal CHIP funds. This fund receives an appropriation separate from the national CHIP allotment amounts. For FY2009, its appropriation was 20% of the CHIP available national allotment. For FY2010 through FY2013, the appropriation will be such sums as are necessary for making payments to eligible states for the fiscal year, as long as the annual payments do not exceed 20% of that fiscal year's CHIP available national allotment. Direct payments from the Contingency Fund can be made to shortfall states for the federal share of expenditures for CHIP children above a target enrollment level.

P.L. 111-148 extends the authority for the Child Enrollment Contingency Fund through FY2015. For FY2013 through FY2015, the appropriation for the Fund will be such sums as are necessary for making payments to eligible states for the fiscal year, as long as the annual payments do not exceed 20% of that fiscal year's CHIP available national allotment. Direct payments from the Contingency Fund can be made to shortfall states for each of FY2013 through FY2015 for the federal share of expenditures for CHIP children above a target enrollment level.

Finally, prior CHIP statute permitted 11 early expansion "qualifying states" to draw some CHIP funds for Medicaid children above 133% of poverty level. P.L. 111-148 extends this authority through FY2015.

Extension of Funding for CHIP through FY2015 and Other Related Provisions

(P.L. 111-148: §10203(a), §10203(b), and §10203(d))

Revisions to the Child Health Quality Measurement Initiative

Under prior law, a child health quality measurement initiative was established for both Medicaid and CHIP. Among several requirements, this initiative includes the establishment of a pediatric quality measurement program that will engage in a number of activities. In general, the purpose of this program is to improve and strengthen core child health quality measures, expand on existing pediatric quality measures used by public and private health care purchasers and advance the development of new and emerging quality measures, and increase the portfolio of evidence- based, consensus pediatric quality measures available to public and private purchasers of children's health services, providers and consumers.

Under P.L. 111-148, the Secretary is required to establish by regulation the criteria for certifying health plans as qualified health plans generally available through the exchange. A number of criteria for such certification are outlined, including, for example, plans must at a minimum utilize a uniform enrollment form for both qualified individuals and employers for enrolling in qualified health plans offered through the exchanges, and utilize a standard format for presenting health plan benefit options. PPACA also requires exchange plans seeking certification to report to the Secretary at least annually (and in a manner specified by the Secretary) these pediatric quality reporting measures.

Participation in, and Premium Assistance for, Employer-Sponsored Health Plans

Under current law states are permitted to purchase family coverage under a group health plan or health insurance that includes CHIP children (through what is called a family coverage variance program), if such coverage is cost-effective relative to (1) the amount of expenditures under the state CHIP plan (including administrative costs) that the state would have made to provide comparable coverage of the children or families involved (as applicable), or (2) the aggregate amount of expenditures that the state would have made under CHIP (including administrative expenses) for providing coverage under the plan for all such children or families. In addition, the coverage must not otherwise substitute for health insurance coverage that would be provided to such children but for the purchase of family coverage, and states must ensure that CHIP minimum benefits are provided, CHIP cost-sharing ceilings are met, and the children to be enrolled have not had group coverage for a specified period of time (typically four to six months)[42]

Under Medicaid law, including a Medicaid expansion CHIP program, states may implement a premium assistance program if the employer plan is comprehensive and cost-effective for the state. Under prior Medicaid law, an individual's enrollment in an employer plan was considered cost-effective if paying the premiums, deductible, coinsurance and other cost-sharing obligations of the employer plan was less expensive than the state's expected cost of directly providing Medicaid-covered services. To meet the comprehensiveness test under Medicaid, current law requires states to provide coverage for those Medicaid-covered services that are not included in the private plans. In other words, states must provide "wrap-around" benefit coverage.

CHIPRA created a new state plan option to offer premium assistance for Medicaid and CHIP- eligible children and/or parents of Medicaid and/or CHIP-eligible children where the family has access to employer-sponsored insurance (ESI) coverage, if the employer pays at least 40% of the total premium, the employer's group health plan qualifies as "creditable coverage"[43] (as defined by the Public Health Service Act), and the coverage is offered to all individuals in a nondiscriminatory way (as defined by the Internal Revenue Code of 1986). Under CHIPRA, a state offering premium assistance may not require CHIP eligible individuals to enroll in an employer's plan; individuals eligible for CHIP and for employment-based coverage may choose to enroll in regular CHIP rather than the premium assistance program. The premium assistance subsidy will generally be the difference between the worker's out-of-pocket premium that included the child(ren) versus only covering the employee. For employer plans that do not meet CHIP benefit requirements, a wrap-around is required. The law also stipulates that the premium assistance provisions under Medicaid, not CHIP, will apply to children enrolled in a Medicaid expansion CHIP program.

Under prior law (as enacted under CHIPRA), for the child's coverage using premium assistance, no cost-effectiveness test was required regarding the cost of the private coverage (plus any necessary wrap-around) relative to regular CHIP coverage. CHIPRA established a separate test for family coverage. If the CHIP cost of covering the entire family in the employer-sponsored plan was less than regular CHIP coverage for the eligible individual(s) alone, then the premium assistance subsidy could be used to pay the entire family's share of the premium.

P.L. 111-148 applies the cost-effectiveness definition used under the CHIP family coverage variance authority to (1) the coverage of Medicaid beneficiaries in employer-sponsored group health plans, (2) the premium assistance option under Medicaid,[44] and to (3) the new CHIPRA state plan option to offer premium assistance for Medicaid and CHIP-eligible children and/or parents of Medicaid and/or CHIP-eligible children.

Definition of CHIP Eligible Children

Section 2110(b) of the Social Security Act defines "targeted low-income child" for CHIP purposes. Generally, such children are not otherwise insured, and live in families with income above Medicaid applicable levels, up to 50 percentage points above that level. (Some states have set higher income standards via waiver authority or by disregarding "blocks of income" in determining financial eligibility, for example). The law also defines two groups of children as being ineligible for CHIP: (1) children who are inmates of public institutions or are patients in an institution for mental disease, and (2) children in families for whom a member is eligible for health benefits coverage under a state health benefits plan through the family member's employment with a public agency in the state.

P.L. 111-148 makes two exceptions to the CHIP exclusion of children of employees of a state public agency. First, children of state employees may be enrolled in CHIP if annual agency expenditures made on behalf of an employee enrolled in a state health plan with dependent coverage (for the most recent state fiscal year) is at least the amount of such expenditures made for state FY1997, adjusted for medical inflation for such preceding year. Second, children of state employees may be enrolled in CHIP if the state determines, on a case-by-case basis, that the annual aggregate amount of premiums and cost-sharing applicable to the family of the child would exceed 5% of the family's income for the year involved.

CHIP Annual Allotments

Prior to PPACA, federal statute provided yearly total allotments for CHIP. Specific annual amounts were appropriated for fiscal years starting with FY1998 ($4.295 billion) through FY2012 ($ 14.982 billion). For FY2013 only, two semi-annual allotments were made available. For the first half of the fiscal year, $2.85 billion was to be available, and for the second half of the fiscal year, another $2.85 billion. In addition, a "one-time appropriation" of $11.706 billion was added to the half-year amounts provided for FY2013. These provisions for FY2013 were intended to annually reduce by the "one-time appropriation" the amount of allotments assumed by the Congressional Budget Office (CBO) for fiscal years after FY2013.

P.L. 111-148 strikes the current law language that provides semi-annual allotments for FY2013, and replaces that language with an appropriation of $17.406 billion for FY2013. The new law also provides an appropriation of $19.147 billion for FY2014, and establishes two semi-annual allotments for FY2015. For the first half of FY2015, $2.85 billion will be made available, and for the second half of FY2015, another $2.85 billion. P.L. 111-148 also modifies this section of the CHIP statute to provide a one-time appropriation of $15.361 billion to be added to the half year amounts provided for FY2015.

Prior law appropriated $100 million in outreach and enrollment grants above and beyond the regular CHIP allotments for FY2009 through FY2013. Ten percent of the allocation is to be directed to a national enrollment campaign, and 10% will be targeted to outreach for Native American children. The remaining 80% is to be distributed among state and local governments and to community-based organizations for purposes of conducting outreach campaigns with a particular focus on rural areas and underserved populations. Grant funds are also targeted at proposals that address cultural and linguistic barriers to enrollment.

P.L. 111-148 expands the time period for the outreach and enrollment grants through FY2015. This provision also changes the appropriation level to $140 million for FY2009 through FY2015.

Technical Corrections to the CHIP Statute

(P.L. 111-148: §2102)

CHIPRA was signed into law on February 4, 2009, to extend and improve CHIP (e.g., to provide federal CHIP allotments to states from FY2009 through FY2013), and for other purposes. The American Recovery and Reinvestment Act of 2009 (ARRA, P.L. 111-5) was signed into law on February 17, 2009, making supplemental appropriations for job preservation and creation, infrastructure investment, energy efficiency and science, assistance to the unemployed, and state and local fiscal stabilization, for fiscal year ending September 30, 2009, and for other purposes.

PPACA corrects selected provisions in CHIPRA and ARRA, including (1) making an adjustment to the FY2010 CHIP allotments for certain previously approved Medicaid expansion programs; (2) clarifying a reference to certain lawfully residing immigrants in CHIP statute; (3) deleting a reference to CHIP funds set aside for coverage of certain Medicaid nonpregnant childless adult waivers when those funds are not expended by September 30, 2011 (this block grant was not included in the final version of P.L. 111-3); (4) for comparing the Current Population Survey (CPS) and the American Community Survey (ACS), using estimates of "high performing states" (i.e., those in the lowest one-third of states in terms of their percentage of uninsured, low-income children); and (5) stipulating that the alternative premiums and cost-sharing provision in Medicaid will not supersede or prevent the application of premium and cost-sharing protections for American Indians under Medicaid and CHIP as established in P.L. 111-5. All of these changes are effective as if they were included in the enactment of P.L. 111-3 and P.L. 111-5.

Miscellaneous

Medicaid Improvement Fund Rescission

(P.L. 111-148: §2007)

In the Supplemental Appropriations Act, 2008 (P.L. 110-252), Congress directed the Secretary to establish a Medicaid Improvement Fund (MIF) to be used by CMS to improve the management of the Medicaid program, including improved oversight of contracts and contractors and evaluation of demonstration projects. MIF funding was to be available in addition to existing

CMS budget authority and was to total $100 million in FY20 14, and $150 million in each FY2015-FY2018. The Medicare, Medicaid, and SCHIP Extension Act of 2007 (MMSEA, P.L. 110-173) revised funding for Physician Assistance and Quality Initiative and these funds were to be used for MIF activities. In December 2009, the Department of Defense Appropriations Act, 2010 (P.L. 111-118) was passed. P.L. 111-118 reduced the amount of funding available for MIF in 2014 from $22.3 billion to $20.7 billion. PPACA rescinds any unobligated MIF funds (as of the date of enactment) for FYs 2014 through 2018.

Removal of Barriers to Providing Home and Community-Based Services

(P.L. 111-148: §2402)

Secretary is required to promulgate regulations to ensure that all states develop service systems designed to (1) allocate resources for services in a manner that is responsive to the changing needs of long-term care beneficiaries receiving home and community-based services and that maximizes their independence; (2) provide the support for such beneficiaries to design an individualized self-directed, community-supported life; and (3) improve coordination among providers to achieve more consistent administration of policies and procedures across federally and state-funded programs, among others.

Funding to Expand State Aging and Disability Resource Centers

(P.L. 111-148: §2405)

Established under the Older Americans Act (OAA), Aging and Disability Resource Centers (ADRCs) provide information and assistance to elderly persons and individuals with physical disabilities, serious mental illness, and/or developmental/intellectual disabilities. ADRCs also serve as a single point of entry for enrollment in publicly administered LTC services, including those funded by Medicaid and OAA. Out of any funds in the Treasury not otherwise appropriated, the law appropriates to the Secretary, acting through the Assistant Secretary of Aging, $10 million for each of FY2010 through FY2014 to carry out ADRC initiatives.

Sense of the Senate Regarding Long-Term Care

(P.L. 111-148: §2406)

The law expresses the sense of the Senate that the 111th Congress should comprehensively address long-term services and supports in a way that guarantees elderly and disabled individuals the care they need, and that makes long term services and supports available in the community as well as in institutions.

Five-Year Period for Dual Eligible Demonstration Projects

(P.L. 111-148: §2601)

Some elderly and disabled individuals, referred to as dual eligibles, qualify for health insurance under both Medicare and Medicaid. These dual eligible individuals qualify for Medicare Part A and/or Parts B and D and are eligible for Medicaid because they have limited income and assets.

Previous federal law gives the Secretary authority to waive selected Medicaid and Medicare requirements, as well as approve waivers to reach individuals who otherwise would be ineligible for Medicaid. Some projects have been approved that waive both Medicare and Medicaid rules to implement statewide initiatives to coordinate service delivery, benefit packages, and reimbursement for dual eligibles. Initially, waivers can be approved for periods ranging from two- to five-year periods and renewed for additional periods of up to five years.

PPACA authorizes the Secretary to initially approve Medicaid waivers for up to five years. This authority applies to demonstrations as well as home and community-based waivers for coordinating care of dual eligibles (and for non dual eligible beneficiaries if they were included under the waiver). In addition, the Secretary has authority to approve Medicaid waiver extensions for additional five-year periods when requested by states, unless the waivers did not meet the conditions for the previous period, or the waiver was no longer cost effective, efficient, or consistent with Medicaid policy.

Federal Coverage and Payment Coordination for Dual Eligible Beneficiaries

(P.L. 111-148: §2602)

There are no specific requirements under previous Medicare and Medicaid law or regulations for the programs to coordinate care for dual eligible individuals. PPACA requires the Secretary to establish a federal coordinated health care office (CHCO) within CMS by March 1, 2010. CMS's Administrator will appoint the CHCO director, who also will report to the CMS Administrator. The CHCO's purpose is to "bring together" Medicare and Medicaid program staff at CMS for purpose of (1) integrating benefits and (2) improving care coordination for dual eligible beneficiaries. The CHCO established under PPACA has the following goals:

1. to provide dual eligible individuals full access to the benefits to which they are entitled under the Medicare and Medicaid programs;
2. to simplify the processes for dual eligible individuals to access the items and services they are entitled to under the Medicare and Medicaid programs;
3. to improve the quality of health care and long-term care services for dual eligible individuals;
4. to increase beneficiaries' understanding of, and satisfaction with, coverage under the Medicare and Medicaid programs;
5. to eliminate regulatory conflicts between rules under the Medicare, and Medicaid programs;
6. to improve care continuity and ensure safe and effective care transitions;
7. to eliminate cost-shifting between the Medicare and Medicaid programs and among related health care providers; and
8. to improve the quality of performance of providers of services and suppliers under the Medicare and Medicaid programs.

PPACA also assigns the CHCO the following specific responsibilities:

1. to provide states, Medicare Advantage plans for special needs individuals, physicians, and other entities or individuals qualified to develop programs, with the education and tools necessary to develop programs that align benefits for duals under Medicare and Medicaid;

2. to support state efforts to coordinate contracting and oversight by states and CMS on the integration of Medicare and Medicaid programs consistent with CHCO goals;
3. to support state and CMS efforts to coordinate contracting and oversight for integrating Medicare and Medicaid programs;
4. to consult with the MedPAC and MACPAC on enrollment and benefit policies for dual eligible individuals; and
5. to study the provision of drug coverage for new full-benefit dual eligibles and to monitor and report on total annual expenditures, health outcomes, and access to benefits for all dual eligibles.

Under PPACA, the Secretary is required to submit a report to Congress under the annual budget transmittal. The report is required to contain recommendations for legislation that could improve care coordination and benefits for dual eligible individuals.

Adult Health Quality Measures

(P.L. 111-148: §2701)

P.L. 111-148 adds a federal initiative to collect and report quality of care data for adults enrolled in Medicaid. Among several activities, the Secretary will publish a recommended core set of adult health quality measures, including such measures in use under public and privately sponsored health care coverage arrangements, or that are part of reporting systems that measure both the presence and duration of health insurance coverage over time. The Secretary is required to publish an initial core set of measures by January 1, 2012. Also, no later than January 1, 2013, the Secretary, in consultation with the states, is required to develop a standardized format for reporting information based on this initial core measurement set. States will be encouraged to use these measures to voluntarily report such data.

As with existing law regarding quality of care reporting for Medicaid children, before January 1, 2014, and every three years thereafter, the Secretary is required to submit a report to Congress that describes the Secretary's efforts to improve, for example, the duration and stability of coverage for adults under Medicaid, the quality of care of different services for such individuals, the status of voluntary state reporting of such data, and any recommendations for legislative changes needed to improve quality of care provided to Medicaid adults.

Within one year after the release of the recommended core set of adult health quality measures, the Secretary is required to establish a Medicaid Quality Measurement Program (MQMP). To this end, the Secretary is required to award grants and contracts for developing, testing, and validating emerging and innovative evidence-based measures applicable to Medicaid adults. Not later than two years after the establishment of the MQMP, the Secretary is required to publish recommended changes to the initial core set of adult health quality measures based on the results of testing, validation, and the consensus process for development of these measures. P.L. 111-148 does not restrict coverage under Medicaid or CHIP to only those services that are evidence-based.

The new law also includes annual state reporting requirements to include, for example, state-specific adult health quality measures, including information collected as part of external quality reviews of managed care organizations and through benchmark plans (if applicable). The Secretary will be required to collect, analyze and make publicly available the information reported by states, before September 30, 2014, and annually thereafter.

Finally, to carry out these activities, P.L. 111-148 appropriates $60 million for each of fiscal years 2010 through 2014. These funds will remain available until expended.

MACPAC Assessment of Policies Affecting All Medicaid Beneficiaries

(P.L. 111-148: §2801, and §10607)

CHIPRA established a new federal commission called the Medicaid and CHIP Payment and Access Commission, or MACPAC. This commission will review program policies under both Medicaid and CHIP affecting children's access to benefits, including (1) payment policies, such as the process for updating fees for different types of providers, payment methodologies, and the impact of these factors on access and quality of care; (2) the interaction of Medicaid and CHIP payment policies with health care delivery generally; and (3) other policies, including those relating to transportation and language barriers. The commission will make recommendations to Congress concerning such payment and access policies. MACPAC is similar to MedPAC which reviews Medicare program policies.

Beginning in 2010, the commission will submit an annual report to Congress containing the results of these reviews and MACPAC's recommendations regarding these policies. The commission will also submit annual reports to Congress containing an examination of issues affecting Medicaid and CHIP, including the implications of changes in health care delivery in the U.S. and in the market for health care services.

MACPAC must also create an early warning system to identify provider shortage areas or other problems that threaten access to care or the health care status of Medicaid and CHIP beneficiaries.

P.L. 111-148 makes a number of changes to the federal statute that established MACPAC. First, the original focus on children will be expanded to include all Medicaid beneficiaries. In addition, MACPAC's review and assessment of payment policies under Medicaid and CHIP will be expanded to include, for example, how factors affecting expenditures and payment methodologies enable beneficiaries to obtain services, affect provider supply, and affect providers that serve a disproportionate share of low-income and other vulnerable populations. Additional topics that MACPAC will be required to review and assess include policies related to eligibility, enrollment and retention, benefits and coverage, quality of care, and interactions between Medicaid and Medicare and how those interactions affect access to services, payments and dual eligibles. MACPAC is also required to report to Congress on any Medicaid and CHIP regulations that affect access, quality and efficiency of health care.

MACPAC must also conduct an independent review of the alternatives to current tort litigation under new state demonstration grants established for this purpose under this new law. This review will assess the impact of such alternatives on the Medicaid and CHIP programs and their beneficiaries, including an analysis of the impact of these alternatives on the efficiency and effectiveness of these two programs. A report on these tort reform activities, including findings and recommendations, is due to Congress no later than December 31, 2016.

In carrying out its duties, MACPAC is authorized to obtain necessary data from any state agency responsible for administering Medicaid or CHIP. The provision of these state data is a condition for receiving federal matching funds under either program. P.L. 111-148 requires MACPAC to seek state input and review state data, and to consider state information in its recommendations and reports. Both MACPAC and MedPAC are required to coordinate and consult with the Federal Coordinated Health Care Office (established under §2081 of this new law) before making recommendations regarding Medicare beneficiaries who are dually eligible. Changes to Medicaid policy affecting dual eligibles are the responsibility of the MACPAC.

For FY2010, P.L. 111-148 appropriates $11 million for MACPAC. Of this total, $9 million will come from the Treasury out of any funds not otherwise appropriated, and $2 million will come from FY20 10 CHIP funds, and will remain available until expended. Funding in subsequent years is not addressed in this provision. This provision is effective upon enactment.

Protections for American Indians and Alaska Natives

(P.L. 111-148: §2901)

The Indian Health Service (IHS), an agency in HHS, provides health care for eligible American Indians/Alaska Natives through a system of programs and facilities located on or near Indian reservations and in certain urban areas. These programs, which may be operated by Indian Tribes (ITs) or Tribal Organization (TOs), are eligible to receive reimbursements from Medicare, Medicaid, CHIP, state programs, and third parties such as private insurance. Facilities are permitted to retain these reimbursements and use them to increase available services.[45] Prior to PPACA, IHS, an IT, or a TO was only considered the payor of last resort for contract health services—services that these facilities purchase through contract, with providers in instances where the facility or program cannot provide the needed care. PPACA designates programs operated by IHS, an IT, TO, or an urban Indian organization (UIO) as the payer of last resort for services provided to eligible American Indians and Alaska Natives, including services covered by Medicaid and CHIP. IHS funds are limited and tribal members have raised concerns about which program is considered the payor of last resort.[46] This provision will clarify such issues, and, as a result, may provide additional funding to programs operated by the IHS, ITs, TOs, or UIOs.

Under a newly permitted option enacted under the Children's Health Insurance Reauthorization Act (CHIPRA, P.L. 111-3), states may facilitate Medicaid enrollment—including under certain conditions, automatically enrolling those eligible—by relying on a finding of eligibility from specified "Express Lane" agencies (e.g., those that administer programs such as Temporary Assistance for Needy Families, Medicaid, CHIP, and food stamps); however, IHS, ITs, TOs, and UIOs were not among the specified "Express Lane" agencies in CHIPRA. American Indians and Alaska Natives face a number of barriers to enrolling in Medicaid and CHIP. GAO found that some tribes have the ability to determine Medicaid eligibility for some of their tribal members, which can facilitate Medicaid enrollment.[47] PPACA permits IHS,

ITs, TOs, and UIOs to serve as "Express Lane" agencies; this may increase Medicaid and CHIP enrollment among American Indians and Alaska Natives.

American Indians and Alaska Natives receiving services through IHS programs or at IHS facilities may not be charged premiums, cost-sharing or similar charges in Medicaid. PPACA also prohibits cost-sharing for American Indians and Alaska Natives enrolled in a qualified health plan offered through the newly established exchanges. American Indians and Alaska Natives are not charged for services provided by IHS, an IT, or a TO.[48] Given this, there may be few incentives to enroll in a private health insurance plan that charges premiums or copayments. This exclusion should facilitate American Indian and Alaska Native enrollment in private health insurance offered through the exchanges.[49]

Establishment of Center for Medicare and Medicaid Innovation within CMS

(P.L. 111-148: §3021 as modified by §10306)

Under Medicaid and Medicaid law, the Secretary has broad authority to develop research and demonstration projects that test new approaches to paying providers, deliver health care services, or provide benefits to Medicare and Medicaid beneficiaries. This section of PPACA requires the Secretary to establish a CMI within CMS by January 1, 2011. The CMI is to test innovative payment and service delivery models to reduce Medicare, Medicaid, and CHIP program expenditures, while preserving or enhancing the quality of care furnished to beneficiaries.

The Secretary is required to identify and select payment and service delivery models that also improve the coordination, quality, and efficiency of health care services. In addition, the Secretary is required to select models that address a defined population for which there are deficits in care leading to poor clinical outcomes, and may include models which allow states to test and evaluate fully integrating care for beneficiaries eligible for both Medicare and Medicaid (dual eligibles), including the management and oversight of all funds, as well as to test and evaluate all-payer payment systems that include dual eligibles. Under PPACA, the Secretary has authority to limit the testing of models to selected geographic areas.

Further, the Secretary is required to conduct an evaluation of each model tested, and make the results of these evaluations available publicly. PPACA appropriated $5 million for the design, implementation, and evaluation of models for FY2010; $10 billion for FY2011 through FY2019; and $10 billion for each subsequent 10 fiscal year period beginning with 2020. Beginning in 2012, and at least every other year thereafter, the Secretary is required to submit a report to Congress on the CMI.

GAO Study and Report on Causes of Action

(P.L. 111-148: §3512)

Under this provision, GAO is required to conduct a study to determine if the development, recognition, or implementation of guidelines or other standards under selected provisions in the law might result in new causes of action or claims. The GAO study will include three Medicaid- related and 11 other non-Medicaid related provisions in the law as shown in **Table 2.**

Table 2. Law Sections to be Included in GAO Study on Causes of Action

Section Number	Section Title
Medicaid Related Provisions	
Sec. 2701	Adult Health Quality Measures
Sec. 2702	Payment Adjustments for Health Care-Acquired Conditions
Sec. 3021	Establishment of Center for Medicare and Medicaid Innovation
Non-Medicaid Provisions	
Sec. 3001	Hospital Value-Based Purchase Program
Sec. 3002	Improvements to the Physician Quality Reporting Initiative (PQRI)
Sec. 3003	Improvements to the Physician Feedback Program
Sec. 3007	Value-based Payment Modifier Under Physician Fee Schedule
Sec. 3008	Payment Adjustment for Conditions Acquired In Hospitals
Sec. 3013	Quality Measure Development
Sec. 3014	Quality Measurement
Sec. 3025	Hospital Readmission Reduction Program
Sec. 3501	Health Care Delivery System Research, Quality Improvement
Sec. 4003	Task Force on Clinical and Preventive Services
Sec. 4301	Research to Optimize Delivery of Public Health Services

Source: PPACA, Titles II, III, and IV, Strengthening Quality, Affordable Health Care for All Americans.

GAO is required to submit the study on causes of action to appropriate congressional committees within two years of enactment of PPACA (March 23, 2012).

Public Awareness of Preventive and Obesity-Related Services

(P.L. 111-148: §4004(i))

The health reform law requires the Secretary to provide guidance and relevant information to states and health care providers regarding preventive and obesity-related services that are available to Medicaid enrollees, including obesity screening and counseling for children and adults. Each state will be required to design a public awareness campaign to educate Medicaid enrollees regarding availability and coverage of such services. The Secretary is required to report to Congress on these efforts, beginning no later than January 1, 2011, and every three years thereafter, through January 1, 2017. The provision authorizes to be appropriated such sums as necessary to carry out these activities.

Section 1115 Waiver Transparency

(P.L. 111-148: §10201)

Section 1115 of the Social Security Act authorizes the Secretary to waive certain statutory requirements for conducting research and demonstration projects that further the goals of Titles Medicaid and CHIP. States submit proposals outlining the terms and conditions of the demonstration program to the Centers for Medicare & Medicaid Services (CMS) for approval prior to implementation. In 1994, CMS issued program guidance that impacts the waiver approval process and includes the procedures states are expected to follow for public involvement in the development of a demonstration project. States were required to provide CMS a written description of their process for public involvement at the time their proposal was submitted.

Public involvement requirements for the waiver approval process continued through the early 2000s. In a letter to state Medicaid directors issued May 3, 2002, CMS listed examples of ways a state may meet requirements for public involvement (e.g., public forums, legislative hearings, a website with information and a link for public comment).

The health reform law imposes statutory requirements regarding transparency in the application and renewal of Medicaid and CHIP Section 1115 demonstration programs that impact eligibility, enrollment, benefits, cost-sharing, or financing. Not later than 180 days after the date of enactment of this subsection, the Secretary is required to promulgate regulations that provide for (1) a process for public notice and comment at the state level, including public hearings, sufficient to ensure a meaningful level of public input; (2) requirements relating to (a) the goals of the program to be implemented or renewed under the demonstration project; (b) the expected state and federal costs and coverage projections of the demonstration project; and (c) the specific plans of the state to ensure that the demonstration project is in compliance with SSA Titles XIX and XXI; (3) a process for providing public notice and comment after the application is received by the Secretary, that is sufficient to ensure a meaningful level of public input; (4) a process for the submission to the Secretary of periodic reports by the state concerning the implementation of the demonstration project; and (5) a process for the periodic evaluation by the Secretary of the demonstration project. The Secretary is required to submit an annual report to Congress concerning actions taken by the Secretary with respect to applications for demonstration projects under this section.

Appendix A. Timeline

This appendix is a timeline of relevant start, end, and deadline dates pertinent to each of the Medicaid and CHIP provisions in P.L. 111-148 and 111-152. Some of the dates describe activities that are to be performed by the Secretary, others are for implementation by states, and still others are relevant to Medicaid and CHIP providers.

The organization of this timeline parallels the organization of this report. Thus, provisions are categorized into six tables, **Table A-1** through **Table A-6**, that match the major issue areas described above. They are eligibility, benefits, financing, program integrity, demonstrations and grant funding, and miscellaneous. Within each table, provisions are ordered by relevant date, with the earliest start, end, and deadline dates presented toward the beginning of each table and the latest start, end, and deadline dates presented toward the end of each table.

Table A-1. Eligibility

Start Date	End Date	Deadline	Provision Title	Provision Description	P.L. 111-148/ P.L. 111-152
March 23, 2010	September 30, 2019		Medicaid Coverage for the Lowest Income Populations (Maintenance of Medicaid income eligibility for Medicaid and CHIP-eligible children)	States are required to maintain current Medicaid and CHIP eligibility standards, methodologies and procedures for children (in effect on March 23, 2010) through 2019 as a condition of receipt of Medicaid federal financial participation.	P.L. 111-148: §2001, §10201 and §10203(c)
March 23, 2010	As determined by the Secretary[a]		Medicaid Coverage for the Lowest Income Populations (Maintenance of Medicaid income eligibility for adults)	States are required to maintain current Medicaid and CHIP eligibility standards, methodologies and procedures for adults (as in effect on March 23, 2010) through 2013 as a condition of receipt of Medicaid federal financial participation.	P.L. 111-148: §2001, §10201
March 23, 2010			State Eligibility Option for Family Planning Services	New optional eligibility category for nonpregnant individuals with income up to the highest level applicable to pregnant women covered under the Medicaid or CHIP state plan or waivers.	P.L. 111-148: §2303

Table A-1. (Continued)

Start Date	End Date	Deadline	Provision Title	Provision Description	P.L. 111-148/ P.L. 111-152
				Presumptive eligibility may apply at state option.	
March 23, 2010			Extension of Funding for CHIP Through Fiscal Year 2015 and Other CHIP-Related Provisions	Regarding CHIP's exclusion of children of state employees, such children can be in CHIP if (1) state expenditures for family coverage in a state plan is at least the amount paid for such costs in SFY1997 (adjusted for medical inflation), or (2) on a case-by-case basis, the state determines that annual, aggregate out-of-pocket spending for coverage exceeds 5% of family income.	P.L. 111-148: §10203(d)(2)(D)
March 23, 2010			Special Rules Relating to Indians (Payer of Last Resort)	Requires that facilities operated by the Indian Health Service, Indian Tribe or Tribal Organization be the payer of last resort for services provided to eligible Indian tribe members.	P.L. 111-148: §2901
March 23, 2010			Special Rules Relating to Indians (Express Lane)	Permits Indian Tribes, Tribal Organizations, and Urban Indian Organizations to serve as Express Lane agencies which determine	P.L. 111-148: §2901

Table A-1. (Continued)

Start Date	End Date	Deadline	Provision Title	Provision Description	P.L. 111-148/ P.L. 111-152
				Medicaid and CHIP eligibility for certain Indian tribal members.	
April 1, 2010[b]			Removal of Barriers to Providing Home and Community-Based Services	New 1915(i) optional eligibility group for persons who require less than an institutional level of care and with income up to 300% of the SSI benefit rate. States can offer different benefit packages to different target groups. New limits are imposed on a state's ability to restrict access to this optional benefit. The Secretary promulgates regulations to ensure that all states allocate resources for LTC services in a manner that is responsive to the changing needs and choices of HCBS beneficiaries, among others.	P.L. 111-148: §2402
October 1, 2010			Inclusion of Information About the Importance of Having a Health Care Power of Attorney in Transition Planning for Children Aging Out of	Requirement that the health care oversight plan developed collaboratively between the state child welfare agency and the state Medicaid agency outline steps to ensure that the health-care related	P.L. 111-148: §2955

Table A-1. (Continued)

Start Date	End Date	Deadline	Provision Title	Provision Description	P.L. 111-148/ P.L. 111-152
			Foster Care and Independent Living Programs	components of the transition plan for youth aging out of foster care are met.	
January 1, 2014	December 31, 2018		Protection for Recipients of Home and Community-Based Services Against Spousal Impoverishment	States are required to apply spousal impoverishment protections when determining eligibility for married individuals applying for certain home and community based services.	P.L. 111-148: §2404
January 1, 2014			Medicaid Coverage for the Lowest Income Populations (New mandatory eligibility group up to 133% FPL)	State requirement to form a new Medicaid eligibility category for all nonelderly, nonpregnant individuals up to 133% FPL. States have the option to begin providing medical assistance to individuals eligible under this new group between April 1, 2010, and January 1, 2014.	P.L. 111-148: §2001, §10201/ P.L. 111-152: §1004 and §1201
January 1, 2014			Medicaid Coverage for the Lowest Income Populations (New minimum income eligibility level raised to 133% FPL for certain	Mandatory minimum income eligibility level for poverty-related children ages 6-18 changes from100% FPL to 133% FPL.	P.L. 111-148: §2001, §10201/ P.L. 111-152:

Table A-1. (Continued)

Start Date	End Date	Deadline	Provision Title	Provision Description	P.L. 111-148/ P.L. 111-152
			Medicaid-eligible children)	(States have the option to implement this change earlier.)	§1004 and §1201
January 1, 2014			Medicaid Coverage for the Lowest Income Populations (New MAGI income counting rule)	States use modified adjusted gross income (MAGI) methodology for determining Medicaid income eligibility for most nonelderly individuals, including certain CHIP-eligible individuals. States have the option to implement this provision earlier.	P.L. 111-148: §2001, §10201/ P.L. 111-152: §1004
January 1, 2014			Medicaid Coverage for the Lowest Income Populations (New optional eligibility group)	States may begin covering all nonelderly, nonpregnant individuals who are otherwise ineligible for a mandatory Medicaid eligibility group and under age 65, with income >133% FPL up to a state-defined income eligibility threshold.	P.L. 111-148: §2001, §10201
January 1, 2014			Permitting Hospitals to Make Presumptive Eligibility Determinations for All Medicaid Eligible Populations	Permits hospitals that participate in Medicaid to make presumptive eligibility determinations for all Medicaid-eligible populations based on guidance established by the Secretary.	P.L. 111-148: §2202

Table A-1. (Continued)

Start Date	End Date	Deadline	Provision Title	Provision Description	P.L. 111-148/ P.L. 111-152
January 1, 2014			Medicaid Coverage for Former Foster Care Children	States are required to cover certain former foster care youth up to age 26.	P.L. 111-148: §2004, §10201
January 1, 2014			Special Rules Relating to Indians (Cost Sharing)	Prohibits cost-sharing for Indian Tribe members enrolled in an exchange plan whose incomes are at or below 300 percent of poverty enrolled in a state exchange.	P.L. 111-148:§2901
		January 1, 2014	Streamlining of Procedures for Enrollment Through an Exchange and State Medicaid, CHIP, and Health Subsidy Programs	State mandate to establish an electronic interface that links Medicaid to state exchange and develops and distributes a standard application form for all state health subsidy programs.	P.L. 111-148: §1413
		January 1, 2014	Enrollment Simplification and Coordination with State Health Insurance Exchanges	Secretary is required to (1) establish a system to ensure that individuals who apply for exchange coverage and are instead found to be eligible for Medicaid or CHIP are automatically enrolled in Medicaid or CHIP, and (2) create a secure electronic interface for the determination of eligibility for medical assistance.	P.L. 111-148: §2201

Table A-1. (Continued)

Start Date	End Date	Deadline	Provision Title	Provision Description	P.L. 111-148/ P.L. 111-152
		January 1, 2015	Medicaid Coverage for the Lowest Income Populations (New state reporting requirements)	New annual state reporting requirements regarding changes in Medicaid enrollment.	P.L. 111-148: §2001(d)(1), §10201
		April 1, 2015	Medicaid Coverage for the Lowest Income Populations (New Congressional reports)	The Secretary must submit new annual reports to Congress on total and new Medicaid enrollment for previous fiscal year.	P.L. 111-148: §2001(d)(2), §10201
Upon Establi-shment of guidance by the Secretary			Medicaid Coverage for the Lowest Income Populations (Presumptive eligibility)	State option to make a presumptive eligibility determination for individuals in the new eligibility category up to 133% FPL or for individuals eligible for family coverage based on guidance established by the Secretary.	P.L. 111-148: §2001, §10201

Note: The term "Secretary" refers to the Secretary of the Department of Health and Human Services unless otherwise specified.

Source: CRS.

a. Through the date the Secretary determines the exchange is fully operational.

b. The first day of the first fiscal year quarter that begins after the date of enactment.

Table A-2. Benefits

Start Date	End Date	Deadline	Provision Deadline Title	Provision Description	P.L. 111-148/ P.L. 111-152
February 4, 2009[a]			Requirement to Offer Premium Assistance for Employer-Sponsored Insurance (State option to offer premium assistance)	State option to offer premium assistance for employer-sponsored insurance (with Medicaid benefit wrap) for Medicaid populations when it is cost-effective to do so.	P.L. 111-148: §2003, §10203
March 23, 2010[b]			Coverage for Freestanding Birth Center Services	Requires Medicaid coverage of care provided in free-standing birthing centers. States are required to separately pay providers administer-ing prenatal, labor and delivery, or postpartum care in such centers.	P.L. 111-148: §2301
March 23, 2010			Scope of Coverage for Children Receiving Hospice Care	Certain children who receive hospice services under Medicaid and CHIP are not required to forgo coverage of services related to the treatment of the child's terminal illness.	P.L. 111-148: §2302
March 23, 2010			Clarification of Definition of Medical Assistance	Clarification of medical assistance definition to include both payments for services provided and the services themselves.	P.L. 111-148: §2304
October 1, 2010			Coverage of Comprehensive Tobacco Cessation Services	States are required to offer counseling and pharmacotherapy to promote cessation of tobacco use by	P.L. 111-148: §4107

Table A-2. (Continued)

Start Date	End Date	Deadline	Provision Deadline Title	Provision Description	P.L. 111-148/ P.L. 111-152
			for Pregnant Women in Medicaid	pregnant women. Cost-sharing for such services is prohibited.[c]	
January 1, 2011			State Option to Provide Health Homes for Enrollees with Chronic Conditions	States can begin offering certain Medicaid enrollees with chronic conditions access to health homes. A 90% FMAP will be paid to states offering health homes for the first 8 fiscal quarters. Secretary may award planning grants to states, not to exceed $25 million, for developing home health programs.	P.L. 111-148: §2703
October 1, 2011			Community First Choice Option (Optional personal care attendant benefit)	States can offer personal care attendant services as an optional state plan benefit to Medicaid beneficiaries whose income does not exceed 150% of FPL, or if greater, certain individuals eligible for institutional level of care.	P.L. 111-148: §240 P.L. 111-152: §1205
October 1, 2011			Community First Choice Option (Financing)	States that choose this option will receive a 6 percentage point FMAP increase for reimbursable expenses.	P.L. 111-148: §2401/ P.L. 111-152: §1205

Table A-2. (Continued)

Start Date	End Date	Deadline	Provision Deadline Title	Provision Description	P.L. 111-148/ P.L. 111-152
January 1, 2013			Improving Access to Preventive Services for Eligible Adults in Medicaid	Regarding current Medicaid option to provide certain clinical preventive services and adult immunizations for adults receiving preventive services without cost-sharing, states will receive a one percentage point increase in their applicable FMAP.	P.L. 111-148: §4106
		December 31, 2013	Community First Choice Option (Report to Congress)	Secretary submits to Congress an interim report evaluating this option.	P.L. 111-148: §2401/ P.L. 111-152 §1205
January 1, 2014			Medicaid Coverage for the Lowest Income Populations (Benchmark and benchmark-equivalent benefit changes)	For applicable eligibility groups, benchmark and benchmark-equivalent benefit packages required to provide at least essential health benefits, such as emergency care, hospitalization and prescription drugs.	P.L. 111-148: §2001(c)
January 1, 2014			State Option to Provide Health Homes for Enrollees with Chronic Conditions (Report requirements)	Secretary contracts to survey participating states and reports to Congress on the program's effects on hospital readmissions, quality improvements, among others.	P.L. 111-148: §2703

Table A-2. (Continued)

Start Date	End Date	Deadline	Provision Deadline Title	Provision Description	P.L. 111-148/ P.L. 111-152
		December 31, 2015	Community First Choice Option	Secretary submits a final report to Congress.	P.L. 111-148: §2401/ P.L. 111-152: §1205
January 1, 2017			State Option to Provide Health Homes for Enrollees with Chronic Conditions (Evaluation to Congress)	Secretary presents an evaluation of this benefit to Congress.	P.L. 111-148: §2703

Note: The term "Secretary" refers to the Secretary of the Department of Health and Human Services unless otherwise specified.

Source: CRS.

a. Effective as if included in P.L. 111-3 (CHIPRA).

b. Effective dates may vary in situations where state legislation is required.

c. FMAP for these services will be increased by one percentage point, beginning January 1, 2013, if states also cover the new optional adult preventive care benefit.

Table A-3. Financing

Start Date	End Date	Deadline	Provision Title	Provision Description	P.L. 111-148/ P.L. 111-152
October 1, 2009	September 30, 2015		Extension of Funding for CHIP Through Fiscal Year 2015 and Other CHIP-Related Provisions	Outreach and enrollment grants are extended through FY2015. Funding for these grants is changed to $140 million for FY2009 through FY2015.	P.L. 111-148: §10203(d)(1), §10203(d)(2)(E)

Table A-3. (Continued)

Start Date	End Date	Deadline	Provision Title	Provision Description	P.L. 111-148/ P.L. 111-152
February 4, 2009[a]	September 30, 2019		Additional Federal Financial Participation for CHIP	New law maintains current CHIP structure and provides appropriations for FY2014 and FY2015. If future appropriations are insufficient, CHIP children will get coverage through state exchanges or Medicaid. If new funding is made available, states will receive a higher enhanced FMAP for CHIP services beginning in FY2016. Beginning January 1, 2014, MAGI will be used to determine eligibility, premiums, and cost-sharing.	P.L. 111-148: §2101, §10203/P.L. 111-152: §1004(b)(2)
February 4, 2009[a]			Technical Corrections (CHIPRA)	Makes corrections regarding (1) certain FY2010 CHIP allotments; (2) a reference in CHIP statue to certain lawfully residing immigrants; and (3) criteria for comparing survey estimates used to identify high performing states.	P.L. 111-152: §2102

Table A-3. (Continued)

Start Date	End Date	Deadline	Provision Title	Provision Description	P.L. 111-148/ P.L. 111-152
February 17, 2009[b]			Technical Corrections (ARRA)	Makes corrections regarding the premium and cost-sharing protections for American Indians under Medicaid and CHIP.	P.L. 111-152: §2102
January 1, 2010			Prescription Drug Rebates (Increased Medicaid Rebates)	Increased the percentage of Medicaid's basic rebate applicable to single source and innovator multiple source outpatient prescription drugs (brand) from 15.1% to 23.1% of average manufacturer price (AMP). Also, increased the basic rebate percentage for non- innovator multiple source outpatient drugs (generic) from 11% to 13% of AMP.	P.L. 111-148: §2501
January 1, 2010			Prescription Drug Rebates (Product Line extensions subject to additional rebate)	New formulations of existing drugs are subject to the additional Medicaid rebate, when applicable, as if they are the original drugs.	P.L. 111-148: §2501
January 1, 2010			Expanded Participation in 340B Program	Adds the following facilities to the list of covered entities eligible to receive discounts through the Public Health Service Act (PHSA)	P.L. 111-148: §7101/P.L. 111-152: §2302

Table A-3. (Continued)

Start Date	End Date	Deadline	Provision Title	Provision Description	P.L. 111-148/ P.L. 111-152
				Sec. 340B program: (1) children's and free-standing cancer hospitals excluded from the Medicare prospective payment system; (2) critical access hospitals; and (3) certain rural referral centers and sole community hospitals.	
March 23, 2010			Prescription Drug Rebates (manufacturers pay rebates for beneficiaries in MMCOs)	Manufacturers that participate in the Medicaid drug rebate program must pay a rebate on drugs pur chased on behalf of beneficiaries enrolled in Medicaid managed care organizations (MMCOs). States are required to report utilization data to manufacturers for beneficiaries enrolled in MMCOs to receive the additional rebates. MMCOs must also report utilization data to states. Drugs purchased under 340B program are exempt from the MMCO rebate.	P.L. 111-148: §2501
September 19, 2010[c]			Improvements to 340B Program Integrity (Improved compliance)	The Secretary must issue regulations on program integrity, the dispute resolution process, and	P.L. 111-148: §7102

Table A-3. (Continued)

Start Date	End Date	Deadline	Provision Title	Provision Description	P.L. 111-148/ P.L. 111-152
				a methodology for calculating ceiling prices.	
October 1, 2010[d]			Providing Adequate Pharmacy Reimbursement	Federal upper payment limits (FULs) for non-innovator, multiple source (generic) drugs are set based on a multiple of 175% of AMP. FULs are applicable to classes where FDA has approved 3 or more therapeutically or pharmacologically equivalent products. The definition of AMP is revised to exclude most discounts, rebates, service fees, and price concessions to wholesalers.	P.L. 111-148: §2503/P.L. 111-152: §1101(c)(3)
January 1, 2011			Special Adjustment to FMAP Determination for Certain States Recovering from a Major Disaster	The FMAP is increased for states that (1) had every county/parish declared by the President as a major disaster area; and (2) for FY2011, had its regular FMAP be at least 3 percentage points lower than the state's highest regular FMAP since FY2008 (excluding the ARRA 6.2% and unemployment adjustments).	P.L. 111-148: §2006

Table A-3. (Continued)

Start Date	End Date	Deadline	Provision Title	Provision Description	P.L. 111-148/ P.L. 111-152
July 1, 2011			Payments to the Territories	Federal FMAP rate for all territories increased from 50% to 55%	P.L. 111-148: §2005, §10201/ P.L. 111-152: §1204
July 1, 2011			Payment Adjustment for Health Care-Acquired Conditions	The Secretary is required to issue regulations to prohibit federal financial participation for health care-acquired conditions, while ensuring that patient access to services is not reduced.	P.L. 111-148: §2702
		September 23, 2011[e]	GAO Study to Make Recommendations on Improving the 340B Program	GAO is required to submit to Congress a report that examines at least the following: (1) whether the 340B program should be expanded; (2) whether mandatory 340B sales of certain products could hinder patients' access to those therapies through any provider; and (3) whether 340B income is being used by covered entities to further program objectives.	P.L. 111-148: §7103

Table A-3. (Continued)

Start Date	End Date	Deadline	Provision Title	Provision Description	P.L. 111-148/ P.L. 111-152
October 1, 2011	September 30, 2015		Incentives for States to Offer HCBS as a Long Term Care Alternative to Nursing Homes	Eligible states that increase their share of Medicaid LTC spending on HCBS to reach 25% of the total, will receive an FMAP increase of 5 percentage points on eligible payments. Other eligible states that increase their share to 50% on HCBS will receive an FMAP increase of 2 percentage points.	P.L. 111-148: §10202
October 1, 2011			Disproportionate Share Hospital (DSH) Payments (Tennessee)	Tennessee receives annual federal DSH allotments to make adjustments to payment rates for certain hospitals. For FY2012 this amount is set at $47.2 million ($30 million per year for FY2009 through FY2011).	P.L. 111-152: §1203
October 1, 2011			Disproportionate Share Hospital (DSH) Payments (Hawaii)	Hawaii receives annual federal DSH allotments to make adjustments to payment rates for certain hospitals. For FY2012 Hawaii will receive $10 million for DSH. This is the same amount as	P.L. 111-148: §2551, §10201(e)

Table A-3. (Continued)

Start Date	End Date	Deadline	Provision Title	Provision Description	P.L. 111-148/ P.L. 111-152
				applied annually for FY2009 though FY2011.	
October 1, 2011			Disproportionate Share Hospital (DSH) Payments	The Secretary must develop a methodology to achieve required annual funding reductions in federal DH payments to states for hospitals.	P.L. 111-148: §2551, §10201(e)/ P.L. 111-152: §1203
October 1, 2012	September 30, 2013		Extension of Funding for CHIP Through Fiscal Year 2015 and Other CHIP- Related Provisions	The new law provides a single appropriation of $17.406 billion for FY2013 for CHIP.	P.L. 111-148: §10203(d)(1), §10203(d)(2)(F)
October 1, 2012			Disproportionate Share Hospital (DSH) Payments (Tennessee)	Tennessee receives annual federal DSH allotments to make adjustments to payment rates for certain hospitals. For FY2013 this amount is set at $52.1million ($30 million per year for FY2009 through FY2011).	P.L. 111-152: §1203
October 1, 2012			Disproportionate Share Hospital (DSH) Payments (Hawaii)	Hawaii receives annual federal DSH allotments to make adjustments to payment rates for certain hospitals. For FY2013 forward, Hawaii is treated as a low	P.L. 111-148: §2551, §10201(e)

Table A-3. (Continued)

Start Date	End Date	Deadline	Provision Title	Provision Description	P.L. 111-148/ P.L. 111-152
				DSH state (i,e., allotments increased by change in CPI-U).	
January 1, 2013	December 31, 2014		Payments to Primary Care Physicians	States must set Medicaid payments for certain primary care services at least equal to Medicare payment rates. For CY2013 and CY2014, FMAP will be 100% for the portion of the new minimum payments that exceeds states' existing payment rates as of July 1, 2009.	P.L. 111-152: §1202
October 1, 2013			Extension of Funding for CHIP Through Fiscal Year 2015 and Other CHIP-Related Provisions	The new law provides an appropriation of $19.147 billion for FY2014.	P.L. 111-148: §10203(d)(1), §10203(d)(2)(F)
		October 1, 2013	Payments to the Territories (Option to create an exchange)	Territories that opt to establish an exchange must submit plan to Secretary for approval by October 1, 2013.	P.L. 111-148: §2005, §10201/ P.L. 111-152: §1204, §1323
January 1, 2014	December 31, 2015		Medicaid Coverage for the Lowest Income Populations (Increased FMAP for Vermont)	Certain expansion states receive 2.2 percentage point increase over regular FMAP for costs associated with prior law eligible populations.	P.L. 111-148: §2001, §10201/P.L. 111-152: §1201

Table A-3. (Continued)

Start Date	End Date	Deadline	Provision Title	Provision Description	P.L. 111-148/ P.L. 111-152
January 1, 2014	December 31, 2016		Medicaid Coverage for the Lowest Income Populations (100% FMAP for "newly eligible" populations in all states)	100% FMAP rate for the cost of providing benchmark and benchmark-equivalent coverage to "newly eligible" populations.	P.L. 111-148: §2001, §10201/ P.L. 111-152: §1201
January 1, 2014	December 31, 2019		Payments to the Territories (Funding for territories that opt to establish an exchange)	$1.0 billion appropriated for the period between 2014 and 2019 for territories with a Secretary approved plan for an exchange.	P.L. 111-148: §2005, §10201/ P.L. 111-152: §1204
January 1, 2014			Elimination of Exclusion of Coverage of Certain Drugs	Smoking cessation agents, including over-the-counter products approved by the Food and Drug Administration, barbiturates, and benzodiazepines would be removed from Medicaid's excluded drug list. States choosing to cover prescription drugs will be required to cover these drugs for most beneficiaries.	P.L. 111-148: §2502

Table A-3. (Continued)

Start Date	End Date	Deadline	Provision Title	Provision Description	P.L. 111-148/ P.L. 111-152
January 1, 2014			Medicaid Coverage for the Lowest Income Populations (Increased FMAP for "expansion states")	Increased federal funding (i.e., transition percentage) for existing childless adult groups in "expansion states." The FMAP rates defined in the "transition percentage" for each such state will vary by year.	P.L. 111-148: §2001, 10201/ P.L. 111-152: §1201
October 1, 2014			Extension of Funding for CHIP Through Fiscal Year 2015 and Other CHIP- Related Provisions	The new law provides an appropriation of $21.061 billion for FY2015.	P.L. 111-148: §10203(d)(1), §10203(d)(2)(F)
January 1, 2017	December 31, 2017		Medicaid Coverage for the Lowest Income Populations (95% FMAP for "newly eligible" populations in all states)	95% FMAP rate for the cost of providing benchmark and benchmark-equivalent coverage to "newly eligible" populations.	P.L. 111-148: §2001, §10201/ P.L. 111-152: §1201
January 1, 2018	December 31, 2018		Medicaid Coverage for the Lowest Income Populations (94% FMAP for "newly eligible" populations in all states)	94% Federal Medical Assistance Payment (FMAP) rate for the cost of providing benchmark and benchmark-equivalent coverage to "newly eligible" populations.	P.L. 111-148: §2001, 10201/ P.L. 111-152: §1201

Table A-3. (Continued)

Start Date	End Date	Deadline	Provision Title	Provision Description	P.L. 111-148/ P.L. 111-152
January 1, 2019	December 31, 2019		Medicaid Coverage for the Lowest Income Populations (93% FMAP)	93% FMAP rate for the cost of providing benchmark and benchmark-equivalent coverage to "newly eligible" populations.	P.L. 111-148: §2001, §10201/ P.L. 111-152: §1201
January 1, 2020			Medicaid Coverage for the Lowest Income Populations (90% FMAP for "newly eligible" populations in all states)	90% Federal Medical Assistance Payment (FMAP) rate for the cost of providing benchmark and benchmark- equivalent coverage to "newly eligible" populations.	P.L. 111-148: §2001, 10201/ P.L. 111-152: §1201

Note: The term "Secretary" refers to the Secretary of the Department of Health and Human Services unless otherwise specified.

Source: CRS.

a. Effective as if included in P.L. 111-3 (CHIPRA).

b. Effective as if included in P.L. 111-5 (The American Recovery and Reinvestment Act (ARRA)—February 17, 2009).

c. Within 180 days of PPACA's enactment date.

d. The first day of the first calendar year quarter beginning at least six months after enactment.

e. Within 18 months of PPACA's enactment date

Table A-4. Program Integrity

Start Date	End Date	Deadline	Provision Title	Provision Description	P.L. 111-148/ P.L. 111-152
Beginning with contract years on or after January 1, 2010			Requirement to Report Expanded Set of Data Elements Under MMIS to Detect Fraud and Abuse (Requirement to submit data to states)	MMCOs are required to submit data to states, including encounter data related to program integrity, oversight, and administration.	P.L. 111-148: §6504
January 1, 2010			Requirement to Report Expanded Set of Data Elements Under MMIS to Detect Fraud and Abuse (requirement to submit data to the Secretary)	States are required to submit to the Secretary additional Medicaid data on program integrity, oversight, and administration.	P.L. 111-148: §6504
March 23, 2010	Date when Infor - mation is made available		Required Disclosure of Ownership and Additional Disclosable Parties Information (Information is to be made available upon Secretary's request)	SNFs and NFs are required to have disclosable party information available upon request by the Secretary, the state where the facility is located, the LTC HHS OIG.	P.L. 111-148: §6101
March 23, 2010			Required Disclosure of Ownership and Additional Disclosable Parties	SNFs and NFs are required to continue reporting all other	P.L. 111-148: §6101

Table A-4. (Continued)

Start Date	End Date	Deadline	Provision Title	Provision Description	P.L. 111-148/ P.L. 111-152
			Information (Continuation of all other reporting requirements)	information required prior to PPACA.	
March 23, 2010			Overpayments	With certain exceptions, PPACA extends the time period for states to repay overpayments due to fraud to one year. The Secretary is required to issue regulations to guide states adapting MMIS edits, conducting audits, or other appropriate actions to identify and correct recurring or ongoing overpayments.	P.L. 111-148: §6506
		September 1, 2010	Mandatory State Use of National Correct Coding Initiative (NCCI)	Secretary is required to identify NCCI methodologies compatible to Medicaid, and to identify new edits applicable only to Medicaid. The Secretary must notify states of applicable NCCI methodologies.	P.L. 111-148: §6507

Table A-4. (Continued)

Start Date	End Date	Deadline	Provision Title	Provision Description	P.L. 111-148/ P.L. 111-152
September 19, 2010[a]			Provider Screening and Other Enrollment Requirements under Medicare, Medicaid, and CHIP	Medicaid, Medicare, and CHIP suppliers and providers being revalidated are subject to additional screening and other enrollment requirements.	P.L. 111-148: §6401, §10603/ P.L. 111-152: §1304
October 1, 2010			Mandatory State Use of National Correct Coding Initiative	Begin using NCCI methodologies applicable to Medicaid.	P.L. 111-148: §6507
		December 31, 2010	Expansion of the Recovery Audit Contractor (RAC) Program	States are required to establish contracts with one or more RACs.	P.L. 111-148: §6411
January 1, 2011			Termination of Provider Participation Under Medicaid if Terminated Under Medicare or Other State Plan(Provider exclusions)	States are required to exclude individuals or entities from Medicaid provider participation if they have unpaid overpayment; are suspended, excluded or terminated from Medicaid or Medicare participation; or are affiliated with individuals or entities who have been terminated.	P.L. 111-148: §6501

Table A-4. (Continued)

Start Date	End Date	Deadline	Provision Title	Provision Description	P.L. 111-148/ P.L. 111-152
January 1, 2011			Medicaid Exclusion From Participation Relating to Certain Ownership, Control, and Management Affiliations	States are required to exclude individuals or entities that have (or have had) ownership, control, or management in an entity that has unpaid or unreturned overpayments, suspensions, or has been excluded or terminated from a Medicaid program (or is affiliated with individuals or entities who were suspended, excluded, or terminated from Medicaid).	P.L. 111-148: §6502
January 1, 2011			Billing Agents, Clearinghouses, or other Alternate Payees Required to Register Under Medicaid	Agents, clearing houses, or other alternate payees that submit Medicaid claims must register with states and the Secretary.	P.L. 111-148: §6503
January 1, 2011			Prohibition on Payments to Institutions or Entities Located Outside of the United States	States are prohibited from making payments for items or services to financial institutions or entities located outside of the U.S.	P.L. 111-148: §6505

Table A-4. (Continued)

Start Date	End Date	Deadline	Provision Title	Provision Description	P.L. 111-148/ P.L. 111-152
		January 1, 2011	Enhanced Medicare and Medicaid Program Integrity Provisions (National Provider Identification requirement)	Regulations and requirement to include National Provider Identification number (NPI) on all claims.	P.L. 111-148: §6402/ P.L. 111-152: §1303
		March 1, 2011	Mandatory State Use of National Correct Coding Initiative	The Secretary must submit a report to Congress on the identification of NCCI edits applicable to Medicaid and on the notice sent to states that identifies Medicaid NCCI edits.	P.L. 111-148: §6507
		March 23, 2011 March 23, 2011	Civil Money Penalties (CMPs)	The Secretary is required to issue regulations governing the reduction and collection of CMPs for SNFs and NFs.	P.L. 111-148: §6111
March 23, 2011			Notification of Facility Closure	SNFs and NFs administrators are required to give at least 60 days notice to the state where the facility is located and the Secretary of their intention to close.	P.L. 111-148: §6113

Table A-4. (Continued)

Start Date	End Date	Deadline	Provision Title	Provision Description	P.L. 111-148/ P.L. 111-152
March 23, 2011			Dementia and Abuse Prevention Training	SNFs and NFs are required to include dementia and abuse prevention training as part of pre-employment initial training for permanent and contract or agency staff.	P.L. 111-148: §6121
March 23, 2011[b]			Provider Screening and Other Enrollment Requirements Under Medicare, Medicaid, and CHIP	New Medicaid, Medicare, and CHIP suppliers and providers are subject to additional screening and other enrollment requirements.	P.L. 111-148: §6401, §10603/ P.L. 111-152: §1304
March 23, 2011	March 23, 2011		National Demonstration Projects on Culture Change and Use of Information Technology in Nursing Homes	The Secretary is required to award demonstration grants for National Demonstration Projects on Culture Change and Use of Information Technology in Nursing Homes.	P.L. 111-148: §6114
		March 23, 2011	Nursing Home Compare Medicare Website	With certain exceptions, the Secretary is required to add additional disclosure information to the Nursing Home Compare Medicare Website.	P.L. 111-148: §6103

Table A-4. (Continued)

Start Date	End Date	Deadline	Provision Title	Provision Description	P.L. 111-148/ P.L. 111-152
		March 23, 2011	Reporting of Expenditures	Secretary is required to consult with private sector accountants to redesign SNF and NF Medicare and Medicaid cost reports to accommodate reporting of direct care expenditures.	P.L. 111-148: §6104
		March 23, 2011	Standardized Complaint Form	The Secretary is required to develop and make available a standardized complaint form to be used by residents (or their representatives) in filing complaints against a SNF or NF.	P.L. 111-148: §6105
		March 23, 2011	National Independent Monitor Demonstration Program	The Secretary is required to develop, test, and implement a an independent two-year monitor demonstration program to oversee interstate and large intrastate chains of SNFs and NFs.	P.L. 111-148: §6112
		December 31, 2011	Accountability Requirements for Skilled Nursing Facilities and Nursing Facilities	The Secretary is required to issue regulations to implement a quality assurance and	P.L. 111-148: §6102

Table A-4. (Continued)

Start Date	End Date	Deadline	Provision Title	Provision Description	P.L. 111-148/ P.L. 111-152
				performance improvement (QAPI) program for SNFs and NFs.	
		December 31, 2011	Accountability Requirements for Skilled Nursing Facilities and Nursing Facilities	The Secretary is required to establish and implement a QAPI program for SNFs and NFs. The Secretary is required to develop QAPI standards and to provide technical assistance to facilities to develop best practices to meet QAPI standards.	P.L. 111-148: §6102
March 23, 2012[c]			Provider Screening and Other Enrollment Requirements Under Medicare, Medicaid, and CHIP	Current Medicaid, Medicare, and CHIP suppliers and providers are subject to additional screening and other enrollment requirements.	P.L. 111-148: §6401,§10603/ P.L. 111-152: §1304
		March 23, 2012	Required Disclosure of Ownership and Additional Disclosable Parties Information (Final regulations from the Secretary)	Secretary is required to issue interim regulations on facility reporting of disclosable party information in a standardized format. SNFs and NFs would not be authorized to dispose or	P.L. 111-148: §6101

Table A-4. (Continued)

Start Date	End Date	Deadline	Provision Title	Provision Description	P.L. 111-148/ P.L. 111-152
				delete disclosable party information available prior to final regulations.	
		March 23, 2012	Accountability Requirements for Skilled Nursing Facilities and Nursing Facilities	Secretary issues SNF and NF regulations identifying requirements for effective compliance and ethics programs.	P.L. 111-148: §6102
		March 23, 2012	Reporting of Expenditures	Facilities (SNFs and NFs) are required to begin reporting direct care staff expenditures on cost reports.	P.L. 111-148: §6104
		March 23, 2012	Ensuring Staffing Accountability	Facilities (SNFs and NFs) are required to begin submitting direct care staff information in a uniform format based on payroll data.	P.L. 111-148: §6106
		March 23, 2012	GAO Study and Report on Five-Star Quality Rating System	The Comptroller General is required to submit a report to Congress on the Five-Star Quality Rating System for SNFs and NFs. The report must include how the system is being implemented, any	P.L. 111-148: §6107

Table A-4. (Continued)

Start Date	End Date	Deadline	Provision Title	Provision Description	P.L. 111-148/ P.L. 111-152
				problems with the system, and how the system could be improved.	
		March 28, 2012[d]	Enhanced Medicare and Medicaid Program Integrity Provisions (Secretary's report)	Secretary required to submit an annual report, which at least identifies the use of funds and the effectiveness of the use of funds.	P.L. 111-148: §6402/ P.L. 111-152: §1303
		June 23, 2012	Required Disclosure of Ownership and Additional Disclosable Parties Information (Final regulations)	Secretary is required to issue final regulations on SNF and NF reporting of disclosable party information in a standardized format	P.L. 111-148: §6101
		September 23, 2012	Reporting of Expenditures	Secretary is required to consult with MedPAC, Medicaid and CHIP Payment Access Commission (MACPAC), HHS OIG, and other experts as determined appropriate to categorize first year expenditure data into functional accounts.	P.L. 111-148: §6104

Table A-4. (Conmtinued)

Start Date	End Date	Deadline	Provision Title	Provision Description	P.L. 111-148/ P.L. 111-152
		December 31, 2012	Accountability Requirements for Skilled Nursing Facilities and Nursing Facilities—Plan to meet Quality Assurance and Performance Improvement Program (QAPI) requirements	SNFs and NFs are required to submit to the Secretary plans for facilities to meet the QAPI requirements	P.L. 111-148: §6102
		March 23, 2013	Required Disclosure of Ownership and Additional Disclosable Parties Information (Additional information to the public)	The Secretary is required to disseminate to the public (as determined by the Secretary) additional SNF and NF disclosable party (e.g., ownership, partnership, and management) information.	P.L. 111-148: §6101
		September 19, 2013	National Independent Monitor Demonstration Program	The Secretary in consultation with HHS OIG is required to evaluate the SNF and NF National Independent Monitor Demonstration Program and submit a report to Congress.	P.L. 111-148: §6112
		March 23, 2014	National Demonstration Projects on Culture Change and Use of Information	The SNF and NF demonstration projects for the National Demonstration Projects on Culture Change	P.L. 111-148: §6114

Table A-4. (Continued)

Start Date	End Date	Deadline	Provision Title	Provision Description	P.L. 111-148/ P.L. 111-152
			Technology in Nursing Homes (Program completion)	and Use of Information Technology in Nursing Homes are to be completed.	
		December 23, 2014	National Demonstration Projects on Culture Change and Use of Information Technology in Nursing Homes (Report to Congress)	The Secretary is required to submit a report to Congress on the National Demonstration Projects on Culture Change and Use of Information Technology in Nursing Homes.	P.L. 111-148: §6114
		March 23, 2015	Accountability Requirements for Skilled Nursing Facilities and Nursing Facilities (Establishment of ethics and compliance programs)	Entities that operate SNFs and NFs are required to have compliance and ethics programs in place that meet the requirements specified by the Secretary.	P.L. 111-148: §6102
		March 23, 2015	Accountability Requirements for Skilled Nursing Facilities and Nursing Facilities (Evaluation to Congress)	The Secretary submits an evaluation report to Congress on compliance and ethics programs for SNFs and NFs.	P.L. 111-148: §6102
March 23, 2010			Enhanced Medicare and Medicaid Program Integrity Provisions (Program evaluation)	Secretary must evaluate program integrity entities with which HHS contracts every three years.	P.L. 111-148: §6402/ P.L. 111-152: §1303

Table A-4. (Continued)

Start Date	End Date	Deadline	Provision Title	Provision Description	P.L. 111-148/ P.L. 111-152
		None specified	Required Disclosure of Ownership and Additional Disclosable Parties Information (Secretarial guidance and technical assistance)	The Secretary is required to provide guidance and technical assistance to states on how to adopt a standard format for reporting additional SNF and NF disclosable party (i.e., ownership, partnership, and management) information.	P.L. 111-148: §6101
		None specified	Enhanced Medicare and Medicaid Program Integrity Provisions (Regulations regarding fraud investigations)	Secretary is required to issue regulations to implement the suspension of Medicare and Medicaid payments pending an investigation of credible fraud allegations.	P.L. 111-148: §6402/ P.L. 111-152: §1303

Note: The term "Secretary" refers to the Secretary of the Department of Health and Human Services unless otherwise specified.

Source: CRS.

a. Effective within 180 days of the date of enactment.

b. Effective one year after the date of enactment.

c. Effective two years after the date of enactment.

d. Effective within 180 days of close of fiscal year (beginning FY2011).

Table A-5. Demonstrations and Grants

Start Date	End Date	Deadline	Provision Title	Provision Description	P.L. 111-148/ P.L. 111-152
October 1, 2009	September 30, 2012		Medicaid Global Payment System Demonstration Project	Participating states adjust payments made to an eligible safety net hospital or network from fee-for service to a global capitated payment model.	P.L. 111-148: §2705
October 1, 2009	September 30, 2014		Funding for Childhood Obesity Demonstration Project	$25 million is appropriated for Childhood obesity demonstration project.	P.L. 111-148: §4306
October 1, 2009	Funds remain available until expended		School-Based Health Centers	New grant program for the establishment (not operation) of school-based health centers that serve large populations of Medicaid and CHIP children. $200 million in total funding for FY2010-FY2013.[a]	P.L. 111-148: §4101
April 22, 2010[b]	September 30, 2016		Money Follows the Person Rebalancing Demonstration	Demonstration is extended.	P.L. 111-148: §2403
April 22, 2010[b]			Money Follows the Person Rebalancing Demonstration	Limits eligibility for demonstration participation to individuals residing in an inpatient facility for not less than 90 consecutive days and excludes Medicare-covered short-term rehabilitative services from counting toward this 90-day period. Removes the maximum length of stay.	P.L. 111-148: §2403
October 1, 2010[c]	December 31, 2015[d]		Medicaid Emergency Psychiatric Demonstration Project	For 3 years, eligible states reimburse certain IMDs for services provided to Medicaid eligibles, age 21 through 64, who require medical assistance to stabilize a psychiatric	P.L. 111-148: §2707

Table A-5. (Continued)

Start Date	End Date	Deadline	Provision Title	Provision Description	P.L. 111-148/ P.L. 111-152
				emergency medical condition. Budget authority of $75 million in advance of appropriations is available.	
January 1, 2011[e]	January 1, 2016[f]		Incentives for Prevention of Chronic Diseases in Medicaid	Secretary awards grants to states to provide incentives for Medicaid enrollees who complete health lifestyle programs.	P.L. 111-148: §4108
January 1, 2012	December 31, 2016		Demonstration Project to Evaluate Integrated Care Around a Hospitalization	Bundled payments are made to hospitals and physicians for the delivery of integrated care during an episode of care that includes a hospitalization.	P.L. 111-148: §2704
January 1, 2012	December 31, 2016		Pediatric Accountable Care Organization Demonstration Project	Pediatric medical providers in participating states will be eligible for incentive payments in exchange for meeting quality performance guidelines and achieving a minimum annual savings level.	P.L. 111-148: §2706
		September 30, 2013	Medicaid Global Payment System Demonstration Project	The Secretary submits to Congress an evaluation report, conducted by the CMS Innovation Center, together with recommendations for legislation and administrative action as the Secretary determines appropriate.	P.L. 111-148: §2705
		January 1, 2014	Incentives for Prevention of Chronic Diseases in Medicaid (Initial evaluation to Congress)	Secretary submits initial evaluation to Congress on the initiatives' effects on service utilization, program participation, and beneficiary satisfaction.	P.L. 111-148: §4108

Table A-5. (Continued)

Start Date	End Date	Deadline	Provision Title	Provision Description	P.L. 111-148/ P.L. 111-152
		July 1, 2016	Incentives for Prevention of Chronic Diseases in Medicaid (Final evaluation to Congress)	Secretary submits final report about whether funding for expanding or extending the initiatives should continue.	P.L. 111-148: §4108
		September 30, 2016	Money Follows the Person Rebalancing Demonstration	Deadline for submission of final evaluation report.	P.L. 111-148: §2403
		December 31, 2017	Demonstration Project to Evaluate Integrated Care Around a Hospitalization (Report to Congress)	The Secretary submits a report to Congress evaluating whether the demonstration lowered costs and improved quality of care.	P.L. 111-148: §2704

Note: The term "Secretary" refers to the Secretary of the Department of Health and Human Services unless otherwise specified.

Source: CRS.

a. $50 million is appropriated for each of FYs 2010 through 2013.

b. This provision is effective 30 days after enactment.

c. Funds become available.

d. Funds remain available for obligation for five years.

e. Law states, or on the date the Secretary develops program criteria, whichever is earlier.

f. Law states, or five years from the date the Secretary develops program criteria.

Table A-6. Miscellaneous

Start Date	End Date	Deadline	Provision Title	Provision Description	P.L. 111-148/ P.L. 111-152
October 1, 2009	September 30, 2010[a]		MACPAC Assessment of Policies Affecting All Medicaid Beneficiaries	Appropriates $11 million for MACPAC. Of this total, $9 million comes from the Treasury out of any funds not otherwise appropriated, and $2 million comes from FY2010 CHIP funds.	P.L. 111-148: §2801/ P.L. 111-152: §10607
October 1, 2009	September 30, 2014		Funding to Expand State Aging and Disability Resource Centers	$10 million appropriated for FY2010-FY2014 for Aging and Disability Resource Centers.	P.L. 111-148: §2405
October 1, 2009	Funds remain available until expended.[b]		Adult Health Quality Measures (AHQM, Financing)	The Secretary establishes adult health quality measures for states to use in their Medicaid programs. Appropriates a total of $300 million for this purpose.	P.L. 111-148: §2701
October 1, 2009			MACPAC Assessment of Policies Affecting All Medicaid Beneficiaries	Broadens the focus of assessment of Medicaid policies affecting all Medicaid beneficiaries (not only children). Also makes a number of changes to CHIPRA, the federal statute that created MACPAC.	P.L. 111-148: §2801/P.L. 111-152: §10607

Table A-6. (Continued)

Start Date	End Date	Deadline	Provision Title	Provision Description	P.L. 111-148/ P.L. 111-152
		March 1, 2010	Providing Federal Coverage and Payment Coordination For Dual Eligible Beneficiaries	Secretary is required to establish a federal coordinated health care office (FCHCO) within CMS.	P.L. 111-148: §2602
March 23, 2010			Medicaid Improvement Fund Rescission (MIF)	Rescinds any unobligated MIF funds for FY2014-FY2018.	P.L. 111-148: §2007
		September 19, 2010	Section 1115 Waiver Transparency	Secretary is required to promulgate regulations regarding transparency in the application and renewal of Medicaid and CHIP Section 1115 demonstration programs.	P.L. 111-148: §10201
January 1, 2011	January 1, 2017		Public Awareness of Preventive and Obesity-Related Services	The Secretary is required to report to Congress by January 1, 2011, on the states' initiatives to increase public awareness of preventive and obesity-related services for Medicaid enrollees. Subsequent reports due every three years.	P.L. 111-148: §4004(i)
		January 1, 2011	Adult Health Quality Measures (Measure publication)	Secretary publishes for comment adult health quality measures for use in state Medicaid programs.	P.L. 111-148: §2701

Table A-6. (Continued)

Start Date	End Date	Deadline	Provision Title	Provision Description	P.L. 111-148/ P.L. 111-152
		January 1, 2011	Establishment of Center for Medicare and Medicaid Innovation (CMI) within CMS	The Secretary is required to establish a Center within CMS that will approve demonstration projects to test payment and delivery models for Medicaid and or Medicare beneficiaries.	P.L. 111-148: §3021,§10306
		February 7, 2011[c]	Providing Federal Coverage and Payment Coordination For Dual Eligible Beneficiaries	Secretary is required to issue a report with recommendations for legislation to improve dual eligible coordination with the annual budget transmission.	P.L. 111-148: §2602
		January 1, 2012	Adult Health Quality Measures (Secretary recommendations)	Secretary recommends core set of adult health quality measures for use in state Medicaid programs.	P.L. 111-148: §2701
		January 1, 2012	Establishment of Center for Medicare and Medicaid Innovation (CMI) within CMS	The Secretary is required to submit a bi-annual report to Congress on the CMI that at least describes the models tested, including the number of individuals that participate, payments made under applicable titles for participating beneficiaries, any models chosen for expansion, and their evaluation results.	P.L. 111-148: §3021, §10306
		March 23, 2012	GAO Study and Report on Causes of Action	GAO is required to submit the study on causes of action in development, recognition, or implementation of	P.L. 111-148: §3512

Table A-6. (Continued)

Start Date	End Date	Deadline	Provision Title	Provision Description	P.L. 111-148/ P.L. 111-152
				guidelines or other standards under selected provisions, to appropriate congressional committees.	
		January 1, 2013	Adult Health Quality Measures (Standardized format for reporting data)	Secretary and states develop standardized format for reporting information based on AHQMs.	P.L. 111-148: §2701
		January 1, 2014	Adult Health Quality Measures (Report to Congress)	Secretary reports to Congress, and every three years thereafter.	P.L. 111-148: §2701
None specified			Five-Year Period for Demonstration Projects	Five-year period for dual eligible demonstration projects with option to extend additional five year periods	P.L. 111-148: §2601
None specified			Extension of Funding for CHIP Through Fiscal FY2015 and Other CHIP-Related Provisions	Exchange plans seeking certification as qualified health plans must report the pediatric quality measures established in CHIPRA (P.L. 111-3) to the Secretary at least annually. First report date not specified	P.L. 111-148: §10203(a)

Note: The term "Secretary" refers to the Secretary of the Department of Health and Human Services unless otherwise specified.

Source: CRS.

a. CHIP funds remain available until expended.

b. $60 million is appropriated for each of FYs 2010 through 2014.

c. This report will be transmitted with the President's budget which can be submitted on or after the first Monday in January, but no later than the first Monday in February.

Appendix B. Statutory References for Medicaid and CHIP Provisions

Table B-1 through **Table B-7** track statutory changes made to the Social Security Act by titles II, IV, VI, and X in P.L. 111-148 and P.L. 111-152. The provision descriptions in the tables are grouped by subject matter into the following categories: eligibility, benefits, financing, program integrity, demonstrations and grant funding, CHIP, and miscellaneous.

Table B-1. The Health Reform Law: Statutory References for Medicaid Changes to Eligibility

Provision	P.L. 111-148		P.L. 111-152
	Title II, Amendments to SSA	**Title X, Amendments to Title II**	**Amendments to P.L. 111-148**
Medicaid Coverage for the Lowest-Income Populations	Sec. 2001	Sec. 10201	Sec. 1004 and Sec. 1201
Financial Eligibility Requirements for 'Newly Eligible' and Other Nonelderly Populations Determined Using Modified Adjusted Gross Income (MAGI)	Sec. 2001	Sec. 10201	Sec. 1004
Financial Eligibility Requirements for Certain Popula-tions Eligible Under Prior Law	Sec. 2001 and Sec. 2002	Sec. 10201	n/a
Medicaid Benefit Coverage for The New Mandatory Eligibility Group	Sec. 2001	Sec. 10201	n/a
Maintenance of Medicaid Income Eligibility (MOE)	Sec. 2001	Sec. 10201	n/a
Medicaid Coverage for Former Foster Care Children	Sec. 2004	Sec. 10201	n/a

Table B-1. (Continued)

Provision	P.L. 111-148		P.L. 111-152
	Title II, Amendments to SSA	Title X, Amendments to Title II	Amendments to P.L. 111-148
Health Care Power of Attorney	Sec. 2955	n/a	n/a
Protection for Recipients of Home and Community-Based Services Against Spousal Impoverishment	Sec. 2404	n/a	n/a
Optional Expansion: Nonelderly, Nonpregnant Individuals with Family Income Above 133% of the FPL	Sec. 2001	Sec. 10201	n/a
Optional Expansion: State Eligibility Option for Family Planning Services	Sec. 2303	n/a	n/a
Optional Expansion: Removal of Barriers to Providing Home and Community- Based Services	Sec. 2402	n/a	n/a
Outreach and Enrollment Facilitation: Streamlining Procedures for Enrollment Through a Health Insurance Exchange and Medicaid, CHIP, and Other Health Subsidy Programs	Sec. 1413	n/a	n/a
Outreach and Enrollment Facilitation: Enrollment Simplification and Coordination with State Health Insurance Exchanges	Sec. 2202	n/a	n/a
Outreach and Enrollment Facilitation: Permitting Hospitals to Make Presumptive Eligibility	Sec. 2202	n/a	n/a

Table B-1. (Continued)

Provision	P.L. 111-148		P.L. 111-152
	Title II, Amendments to SSA	Title X, Amendments to Title II	Amendments to P.L. 111-148
Determinations for All Medicaid Eligible Populations			
Outreach and Enrollment Facilitation: Standard and Best Practices to Improve Enrollment of Vulnerable and Undeserved Populations	Sec. 2201	n/a	n/a
Outreach and Enrollment Facilitation: New Reporting Requirements	Sec. 2001	Sec.10201	n/a

Source: Prepared by CRS based on provisions in P.L. 111-148, as amended by P.L. 111-152.

Table B-2. The Health Reform Law: Statutory References for Medicaid Changes to Benefits

Provision	P.L. 111-148		P.L. 111-152
	Title II, IV, Amendments to SSA	Title X, Amendments to Title II, IV	Amendments to P.L. 111-148
Modifications to DRA Benchmark and Benchmark-Equivalent Coverage	Sec. 2001(c)	n/a	n/a
Premium Assistance	Sec. 2003	Sec. 10203(b)	n/a
Birthing Centers	Sec. 2301	n/a	n/a

Table B-2. (Continued)

Provision	P.L. 111-148		P.L. 111-152
	Title II, IV, Amendments to SSA	**Title X, Amendments to Title II, IV**	**Amendments to P.L. 111-148**
Smoking Cessation Services for Pregnant Women	Sec. 4107	n/a	n/a
Adult Preventive Care	Sec. 4106	n/a	n/.a
Scope of Coverage for Children Receiving Hospice Care	Sec. 2302	n/a	n/a
Community First Choice Option	Sec. 2401	n/a	n/a
State Option to Provide Health Homes for Enrollees with Chronic Conditions	Sec. 2703	n/a	n/a
Changes to Existing Medicaid Benefits: Removal of Barriers to providing Home Community- Based Services	Sec. 2402	n/a	n/a
Changes to Existing Medicaid Benefits: Clarification of the Definition of Medical Assistance	Sec. 2304	n/a	n/a

Source: Prepared by CRS based on provisions in P.L. 111-148, as amended by P.L. 111-152.

Table B-3. The Health Reform Law: Statutory References for Medicaid Changes to Financing

Provision	P.L. 111-148		P.L. 111-152
	Title II, Amendments to SSA	**Title X, Amendments to Title II**	**Amendments to P.L. 111-148**
Payments to States: Additional Federal Financial Assistance Under Health Reform	Sec. 2001	Sec. 10201	Sec. 1201 and Sec. 1202
Payments to States: Incentives for States to Offer Home and Community-Based Services as Long-Term Care Alternative to Nursing Homes	n/a	Sec. 10202	n/a
Payments to States: Disproportionate Share Hospital Payments	Sec. 2551	Sec.10201(e)	Sec. 1203
Payments to States: Special FMAP Adjustment for States Recovering from a Major Disaster	Sec. 2006	n/a	n/a
Payments to The Territories	Sec. 2005	Sec. 10201	Sec. 1204
Payments for Primary Care Providers	n/a	n/a	Sec. 1202
Payments to Providers for Health Care- Acquired Conditions	Sec. 2702	n/a	n/a
Prescription Drugs: Prescription Drug Rebates	Sec. 2501	n/a	n/a
Prescription Drugs: Elimination of Exclusion of Coverage of Certain Drugs	Sec. 2502	n/a	n/a
Prescription Drugs: Providing Adequate Pharmacy Reimbursement	Sec. 2503	n/a	n/a
Prescription Drugs: 340B Prescription Drug Discount Program Expansion	Sec. 7101-7103	n/a	Sec. 2302

Source: Prepared by CRS based on provisions in P.L. 111-148, as amended by P.L. 111-152.

Table B-4. The Health Reform Law: Statutory References for CHIP and Medicaid Changes to Program Integrity

Provision	P.L. 111-148		P.L. 111-152
	Title VI, Amendments to SSA	Title X, Amendments to Title VI	Amendments to P.L. 111-148
Expansion of the Recovery Audit Contractor (RAC) Program	Sec. 6411	n/a	n/a
Termination of Provider Participation Under Medicaid of Other State Health Care Program	Sec. 6501	n/a	n/a
Medicaid Exclusion from Participation Relating to Certain Ownership, Control, and Management Affiliations	Sec. 6502	n/a	n/a
Billing Agents, Clearinghouses, or Other Alternate Payees Required to Register Under Medicaid	Sec. 6503	n/a	n/a
Requirement to Report Expanded Set of Data Elements Under MMIS to Detect Fraud and Abuse	Sec. 6504	n/a	n/a
Prohibition on Payments to Institutions or Entities Located Outside of the United Sates	Sec. 6505	n/a	n/a
Overpayments	Sec. 6506	n/a	n/a
Mandatory State Use of National Correct Coding Initiatives	Sec. 6507	n/a	n/a
General Effective Date for Medicaid and CHIP Program Integrity Activities	Sec. 6508	n/a	n/a
Other Program Integrity and Related Provisions Applicable to Medicaid: Provider Screening and Other Enrollment Requirements under Medicare, Medicaid and CHIP	Sec. 6401	Sec. 10603	n/a

Table B-4. (Continued)

Provision	P.L. 111-148		P.L. 111-152
	Title VI, Amendments to SSA	**Title X, Amendments to Title VI**	**Amendments to P.L. 111-148**
Other Program Integrity and Related Provisions Applicable to Medicaid: Enhanced Medicare and Medicaid Program Integrity Provisions	Sec. 6402	n/a	Sec. 1302
Other Program Integrity and Related Provisions Applicable to Medicaid: Improving Nursing Home Transparency, Enforcement and Staff Training	Sec. 6101-6107 Sec. 6111-6114 Sec. 6121	n/a	n/a

Source: Prepared by CRS based on provisions in P.L. 111-148, as amended by P.L. 111-152.

Table B-5. The Health Reform Law: Statutory References for Medicaid Changes to Demonstrations and Grant Funding

Provision	P.L. 111-148		P.L. 111-152
	Title II, IV, Amendments to SSA	**Title X, Amendments to Title II, IV**	**Amendments to P.L. 111-148**
Money Follows the Person	Sec. 2403	n/a	n/a
Demonstration Project to Evaluate Integrated Care Around Hospitalization	Sec. 2704	n/a	n/a
Medicaid Global Payment System Demonstration Project	Sec. 2705	n/a	n/a

Table B-5. (Continued)

Provision	P.L. 111-148		P.L. 111-152
	Title II, IV, Amendments to SSA	Title X, Amendments to Title II, IV	Amendments to P.L. 111-148
Pediatric Accountable Care Organization Demonstration Project	Sec. 2706	n/a	n/a
Medicaid Emergency Psychiatric Demonstration Project	Sec. 2707	n/a	n/a
Grants for School-Based Health Centers	Sec. 4104(a)	n/a	n/a
Grants for Prevention of Chronic Disease	Sec. 4108	n/a	n/a
Funding of Childhood Obesity Demonstration Project	Sec. 4306	n/a	n/a

Source: Prepared by CRS based on provisions in P.L. 111-148, as amended by P.L. 111-152.

Table B-6. The Health Reform Law: Statutory References for Changes to CHIP

Provision	P.L. 111-148		P.L. 111-152
	Title II, Amendments to SSA	Title X, Amendments to Title II	Amendments to P.L. 111-148
Additional Federal Financing Participation for CHIP	Sec. 2101	Sec. 10203(c)	n/a
Distribution of CHIP allotments Among States	Sec. 2101	Sec. 10203(d)	n/a
Extension of Funding for CHIP Through FY2015 and Other Related Provisions	n/a	Sec. 10203(a) Sec. 10203(b) Sec. 10202(d)	n/a

Source: Prepared by CRS based on provisions in P.L. 111-148, as amended by P.L. 111-152.

Table B-7. The Health Reform Law: Statutory References for Miscellaneous Changes to Medicaid

Provision	P.L. 111-148		P.L. 111-152
	Title II, Amendments to SSA	Title X, Amendments to Title II	Amendments to P.L. 111-148
Medicaid Improvement Fund Rescission	Sec. 2007	n/a	n/a
Removal of Barriers to Providing Home and Community- Based Services	Sec. 2402	n/a	n/a
Funding to Expand State Aging and Disability Resource Centers	Sec. 2405	n/a	n/a
Sense of the Senate Regarding Long-Term Care	Sec. 2406	n/a	n/a
Five-Year Period for [Dual Eligible] Demonstration Projects	Sec. 2601	n/a	n/a
Federal Coverage and Payment Coordination for Dual Eligible Beneficiaries	Sec. 2602	n/a	n/a
Adult Health Quality Measures	Sec. 2701	n/a	n/a
MACPAC Assessment of Policies Affecting All Medicaid Beneficiaries	Sec. 2801 Sec. 399V-4	n/a	n/a
Protections for American Indians and Alaska Natives	Sec. 2901	n/a	n/a
Establishment of Center for Medicare and Medicaid Innovation within CMS	Sec. 3021	Sec. 10306	n/a
GAO Study and Report on Causes of Action	Sec. 3512	Sec. 3512	n/a
Public Awareness of Preventive and Obesity-Related Services	Sec. 4004(i)	n/a	n/a
Section 1115 Waiver Transparency	n/a	Sec. 10201	n/a

Source: Prepared by CRS based on provisions in P.L. 111-148, as amended by P.L. 111-152.

Appendix C. List of Abbreviations and Their Definitions

ACIP	Advisory Committee on Immunization Practices
ACO	Accountable Care Organization
ADHC	Adult Day Health Care
ADL	Activity of Daily Living
ADRC	Aging and Disability Resource Center
AFDC	Aid to Families with Dependent Children
AMP	Average Manufacture Price
ARRA	American Recovery and Reinvestment Act of 2009
ASP	Average Sales Price
BBA	Balanced Budget Act of 1997
BIA	Bureau of Indian Affairs
BMI	Body Mass Index
CBO	Congressional Budget Office
CCI	Correct Coding Initiative
CDC	Centers for Disease Control and Prevention
CFCIP	Chafee Foster Care Independence Program
CFR	Code of Federal Regulations
CG	Comptroller General of the United States
CHCO	Coordinated Health Care Office
CHIP	Children's Health Insurance Program
CHIRPA	Children's Health Insurance Program Reauthorization Act of 2009
CLASS	Community Living Assistance Services and Supports
CMI	Center for Medicare and Medicaid Innovation
CMP	Civil Monetary Penalties
CMS	Center for Medicare and Medicaid Services
CoPs	Conditions of Participation
CPI	Consumer Price Index
CPI-U	Consumer Price Index for Urban Consumers
CPS	Current Population Survey
CRIPA	Civil Rights of Institutionalized Persons Act
DME	Durable Medical Equipment
DOD	Department of Defense
DOJ	Department of Justice
DRA	Deficit Reduction Act of 2005

DRG	Diagnosis-related Group
DSH	Disproportionate Share Hospitals
E & M	Evaluation and Management
E-FMAP	Enhanced FMAP
EPHI	Protected Health Information in Electronic Form
EPSDT	Early and Periodic Screening, Diagnostic and Treatment
ESI	Employer Sponsored Insurance
FCA	False Claims Act
FDA	Food and Drug Administration
FEHBP	Federal Employees Health Benefits Program
FERA	Fraud Enforcement and Recovery Act of 2009
FFP	Federal Financial Participation
FFS	Fee for Service
FMAP	Federal Medical Assistance Percentage
FPL	Federal Poverty Level
FQHC	Federally Qualified Health Centers
FUL	Federal Upper Payment Limit
FY	Fiscal Year
GAO	Government Accountability Office
GME	Graduate Medical Education
GSA	Government Services Administration
HAC	Hospital Acquired Condition
HCBS	Home and Community-Based Services
HCFAC	Health Care Fraud and Abuse Control
HCERA	Health Care and Education Reconciliation Act of 2010
HH	Home Health
HHS	Department of Health and Human Services
HIPDB	Healthcare Integrity and Protection Databank
HIPPA	Health Insurance Portability and Accountability Act of 1996
HMO	Health Maintenance Organization
HRSA	Health Resources and Services Administration
IADL	Instrumental Activity of Daily Living
ICF/MR	Intermediate Care Facility for the Mentally Retarded
IDR	Integrated Data Repository
HIS	Indian Health Services
IMD	Institutions for Mental Disease
IRC	Internal Revenue Code
IT	Indian Tribe

JTC	Joint Committee on Taxation
LEI	List of Excluded Individuals
LEIE	List of Excluded Individuals/Entities
LIS	Low-Income Subsidy
LTC	Long-Term Care
MA	Medicare Advantage
MAC	Medicaid Acquisition Costs
MACPAC	Medicaid and CHIP Payment and Access Commission
MedPAC	Medicare Payment Advisory Commission
MCO	Managed Care Organization
MFCU	Medicaid Fraud Control Units
MFP	Money Follows the Person
MAGI	Modified Adjusted Gross Income
MIF	Medicaid Improvement Fund
MIP	Medicaid Integrity Program
MIPPA	Medicare Improvements for Patients and Providers Act of 2008
MMA	Medicare Prescription Drug, Improvement, and Modernization Act of 2003
MMCO	Medicaid Managed Care Organization
MMIS	Medicaid Management Information System
MMSEA	Medicare, Medicaid, and SCHIP Extension Act of 2007
MOE	Medicaid Eligibility Maintenance of Effort
MOU	Memorandum of Understanding
MQMP	Medicaid Quality Measurement Program
MSIS	Medicaid Statistical Information System
MSP	Medicare Savings Program
NCCI	National Correct Coding Initiative
NDC	National Drug Code
NF	Nursing Facility
NPDB	National Practitioner Databank
NPI	National Provider Identifier
O/PDECP	Office or Program of Dual Eligible Coordination and Protection
OAA	Older Americans Act
OACT	Office of the Chief Actuary
OIG	Office of Inspector General
OMB	Office of Management and Budget
OTC	Over-the-Counter

PACE	Programs of All-inclusive Care for the Elderly
PAQI	Physician Assistance and Quality Initiative
PDP	Prescription Drug Plan
PECOS	Provider Enrollment, Chain and Ownership System
PHI	Protected Health Information
PHSA	Public Health Service Act
PPACA	Patient Protection and Affordable Care Act
PPS	Prospective Payment System
PRWORA	Personal Responsibility and Work Opportunity Reconciliation Act of 1996
QI	Qualifying Individual
QIO	Medicare Quality Improvement Organizations
QMBs	Qualified Medicare Beneficiaries
RAC	Recovery Audit Contractor
RHC	Rural Health Clinic
SBHC	School-Based Health Clinic
SFY	State Fiscal Year
SLMB	Specified Low-Income Medicare Beneficiaries
SNF	Skilled Nursing Facilities
SPA	State Plan Amendment
SSA	Social Security Act
SSI	Supplemental Security Income
STC	Special Terms and Conditions
TANF	Temporary Assistance to Needy Families
TFC	Therapeutic Foster Care
TMA	Transitional Medical Assistance
TO	Tribal Organization
TRHCA	Tax Relief and Health Care Act
UIO	Urban Indian Organization
USC	United States Code
USPSTF	United States Preventive Services Task Force
VA	Department of Veterans Affairs
VFC	Vaccines for Children

End Notes

[1] Congressional Budget Office, letter to Honorable Nancy Pelosi, March 20, 2010, available at http://www.cbo.gov/ftpdocs/ 113xx/doc11379/ Manager's Amendmentto Reconciliation Proposal. pdf.

[2] Congressional Budget Office, letter to the Honorable Harry Reid, March 11, 2010, available at http://www.cbo.gov/ftpdocs/113xx/doc11307/Reid_Letter_HR3590.pdf.

[3] For individuals whose income will be determined using the new income counting rules, the law also specifies that an income disregard in the amount of 5% FPL be deducted from an individual's income when determining Medicaid eligibility. This income counting rule effectively raises the upper income eligibility threshold for the new Medicaid eligibility group to 138% FPL.

[4] For a description of the exchanges, see CRS Report R40942, *Private Health Insurance Provisions in the Patient Protection and Affordable Care Act (PPACA)*, by Hinda Chaikind et al.

[5] Unlike most other eligibility groups, medical expenses (if any) may be subtracted from income in determining financial eligibility for medically needy coverage. This is often referred to as "spend down."

[6] Similar to existing state health reform models, such as the Massachusetts Connector, the Exchange will facilitate the purchase of qualified health benefit plans by individuals and businesses. The Exchange will not be a health insurer; but will provide eligible individuals and small businesses a vehicle to shop and compare insurers' health plans.

[7] Congressional Budget Office, letter to Honorable Nancy Pelosi, March 20, 2010, available at http://www.cbo.gov/ ftpdocs/1 13xx/doc1 1379/Manager'sAmendmenttoReconciliationProposal.pdf.

[8] Certain people with disabilities or other conditions who come into Medicaid through this new eligibility group may be subject to different income counting rules. Official guidance from CMS about who, if anyone, might be exempt from MAGI rules for this new mandatory eligibility pathway has not yet been released.

[9] When calculating income eligibility based on MAGI, Section 1004(e) of HECRA requires states to apply an income disregard equal to the dollar amount equivalent (expressed as a percentage of the federal poverty line) to the difference between the income eligibility threshold applicable to that group and an increase in such threshold by 5 percentage points.

[10] Center for Medicare and Medicaid Services, Center for Medicaid and State Operations, letter to state health officials and state Medicaid Directors (SMDL# 10-005, PPACA #1), *New Option for Coverage of Individuals Under Medicaid,* April 9, 2010.

[11] Section 1931 of the Social Security Act, added in 1996, allows states to cover low income parents with incomes below Aid to Families with Dependent Children 1996 thresholds. States may provide coverage to parents with higher incomes by increasing asset and income limits and utilizing asset and income disregards.

[12] MAGI will be used for determining the amount of premium credit assistance for the purchase of a qualified health benefits plan under state exchanges, described in Section 1401 of PPACA. For more information on MAGI see CRS Report R40942, *Private Health Insurance Provisions in the Patient Protection and Affordable Care Act (PPACA)*, by Hinda Chaikind et al. The transition to MAGI under Medicaid will help with the coordination between state exchanges and Medicaid that is also required under PPACA.

[13] Long term care services include institutional services, such as nursing facility care and home or community-based services, such as home care, personal care, transportation, and care management, furnished under the state plan or a waiver.

[14] Benchmark rules apply to states that opt to expand coverage to the new eligibility group (prior to 2014) and at the point that the eligibility group is mandatory for all states (after 2014) regardless of whether the state has otherwise elected the DRA option to provide benchmark

benefit coverage under its state plan. Center for Medicare and Medicaid Services, Center for Medicaid and State Operations, letter to state health officials and state Medicaid Directors (SMDL# 10-005, PPACA #1), *New Option for Coverage of Individuals Under Medicaid*, April 9, 2010.

[15] Section 2101 P.L. 111-148 contains a CHIP MOE provision. Upon enactment, states would be required to maintain income eligibility levels for CHIP through September 30, 2019, as a condition of receiving payments *under Medicaid*. Specifically, with the exception of waiting lists for enrolling children in CHIP or enrolling CHIP-eligible children in certified exchange plans, states could not implement eligibility standards, methodologies, or procedures that are more restrictive than those in place on the date of enactment. However, states could expand their current income eligibility levels—that is, states could enact less restrictive standards, methodologies or procedures. For more information on the State Children's Health Insurance Program, see CRS Report R40444, *State Children's Health Insurance Program (CHIP): A Brief Overview*, by Elicia J. Herz, Chris L. Peterson, and Evelyne P. Baumrucker.

[16] During the transition to MAGI, the provision directs states to work with the Secretary to establish an equivalent income test that ensures that individuals eligible for Medicaid services as of the date of enactment will not lose coverage. The language in this part of the provision conflicts with the earlier MOE language whereby states are only required to maintain their current Medicaid and CHIP eligibility methodologies, thresholds, and procedures for adults through 2013 (or when the Secretary determines that the state exchange is fully operational).

[17] For more information on benchmark and benchmark-equivalent coverage, including the recently enacted changes to this coverage, see the Benefits section of this report.

[18] For individuals whose income will be determined using MAGI, the law also specifies that an income disregard in the amount of 5% FPL be deducted from an individual's income when determining Medicaid eligibility.

[19] For more information on benchmark and benchmark-equivalent coverage, including the recently enacted changes to this coverage, see the "Benefits" section of this report.

[20] Department of Health and Human Services, Centers for Medicare and Medicaid Services (CMS), Medicaid Program: States Flexibility for Medicaid Benefit Packages, Final Rule, 75 *Federal Register* 23068 (April 30, 2010).

[21] Some of these essential health benefits were already required under these plans prior to PPACA. In addition, essential health benefits are also required of plans in the individual and small group markets under PPACA.

[22] The cost effectiveness test for Medicaid state plan option for premium assistance for children was modified under P.L. 111-148: §10203(b).

[23] States will be allowed to continue to exclude coverage of agents to promote smoking cessation for other Medicaid beneficiaries, as permitted in prior law.

[24] 50% in 2014, 60% in 2015, 70% in 2016, 80% in 2018, and 100% thereafter.

[25] Federal financial participation for some of the Medicaid benefit-related provisions under PPACA (e.g., adult preventive care, tobacco cessation services for pregnant women) are tied to the FMAP rates states will receive for "newly eligible" populations. Federal financial participation for these provisions will also be impacted by the proposed changes to the FMAP rates for "newly eligible" populations under the reconciliation bill.

[26] FY2011 FMAP rates for all states are available at http://aspe.hhs.gov/health

[27] For more information on the federal medical assistance percentage (FMAP), see CRS Report RL32950, *Medicaid: The Federal Medical Assistance Percentage (FMAP)*, by April Grady and Chris L. Peterson.

[28] In creating the HAC program, the Secretary was to select conditions that (1) were high cost, high volume, or both; resulted in the assignment of a case to a DRG that has a higher payment when present as a secondary diagnosis; and were reasonably preventable through the application of evidence-based guidelines.

[29] These preventable errors are sometimes called "never events." Never events include surgery on the wrong body part or mismatched blood transfusions which can cause serious injury or death to beneficiaries and result in increased costs to the Medicare program to treat the consequences of the error.

[30] See State Medicaid Director Letter, SMDL #08-004, July 31, 2008, at http://www.cms.hhs.gov/SMDL/downloads/ SMD073 108.pdf.

[31] Selected drug purchases are exempted from the calculation of state Medicaid rebates, such as drugs dispensed by Medicaid managed care organizations (when prescription drugs are included in the capitation agreement), inpatient drugs, and drugs dispensed in physicians' or dentists' offices (for Medicaid beneficiaries). Some states exclude or carve out drug benefits from their Medicaid MCO contracts, in which case, managed care beneficiaries receive their prescribed drugs through the fee-for-service delivery system, and states can claim manufacturer rebates for these purchases.

[32] Testimony of Dennis Smith, Director, Center for Medicaid and State Operations, Centers for Medicare and Medicaid Services, before the House Energy and Commerce Committee, Subcommittee on Oversight and Investigations, December 7, 2004.

[33] States will receive a rebate of 17.1% for certain outpatient single source and innovator multiple source drugs. These drugs include clotting factor drugs and outpatient drugs approved by the Food and Drug Administration exclusively for pediatric indications.

[34] New orphan drug formulations are exempted from the additional rebate requirements, regardless of whether the market exclusivity period has expired. Orphan drugs, as designated by Sec. 526 of the Federal Food, Drug, and Cosmetic Act, are used to treat individuals suffering from rare diseases.

[35] FULs are set for pharmaceutically and therapeutically equivalent multiple source drugs available nationally through commercial pharmacies.

[36] For more information on the PHSA Sec. 340B provisions, see CRS Report R40943, *Public Health, Workforce, Quality, and Related Provisions in the Patient Protection and Affordable Care Act (P.L. 111-148)*, coordinated by C. Stephen Redhead and Erin D. Williams.

[37] PPACA expanded 340B discounts to inpatient drugs for hospital entities, but this provision was repealed in HCERA. Similarly, PPACA required hospital entities to issue credits to Medicaid programs for inpatient drugs purchased for Medicaid beneficiaries. This provision was also repealed in HCERA.

[38] Safety net hospitals are defined as hospitals that accept patients regardless of their ability to pay, and a substantial share of their patient mix consists of the uninsured and Medicaid patients.

[39] For information about this related provision, see CRS Report R40943, *Public Health, Workforce, Quality, and Related Provisions in the Patient Protection and Affordable Care Act (P.L. 111-148)*, coordinated by C. Stephen Redhead and Erin D. Williams.

[40] Certain expenditures include translation services, CHIP-enrolled children above 300% FPL outside New Jersey and New York, expenditures for administration of citizenship documentation/verification, expenditures for administration of payment error rate measurement or PERM, and Medicaid coverage of certain breast or cervical cancer patients.

[41] For the FY2009 allotment formula, the state's growth factor, called the "allotment increase factor," was the product of (a) 1 plus the percentage increase (if any) in the projected per capita spending in the National Health Expenditures for 2009 over 2008, and (b) 1.01 plus the percentage change in the child population in each state (except for the territories, for which the national amount is used) from July 1, 2008, to July 1, 2009, based on the most recent published estimates of the Census Bureau. For future fiscal years, the growth factor is calculated in the same way, but uses updated projected per capita spending in the National Health Expenditures for each such fiscal year, and the percentage change in the child population in each state (except for the territories, for which the national amount is used)

from July 1 of the previous calendar year, to July 1 of the applicable calendar year, based on the most recent published estimates of the Census Bureau.

[42] CHIP premium assistance programs approved under state plan authority are referred to as family coverage variance programs. As of June 7, 2007, there were two states—New Jersey and Massachusetts—with operational family coverage variance programs under CHIP.

[43] Benefits provided under a health flexible spending arrangement or a high deductible health plan are specifically excluded as credible health coverage under CHIPRA.

[44] Effective January 1, 2014, Section 1906A of the Social Security Act to permit states to offer premium assistance subsidies for children will be broadened to include the parents of such children.

[45] CRS Report R41 152, *Indian Health Care Improvement Act Provisions in the Patient Protection and Affordable Care Act (PPACA)*, by Elayne J. Heisler and Roger Walke. PPACA makes a number of changes to health care provided by IHS, ITs, and TOs within the Indian Health Care Improvement provisions within the bill. Provisions described in this report may also relate to these facilities receiving reimbursements from Medicaid and CHIP.

[46] U.S. Congress, Senate Committee on Indian Affairs, OVERSIGHT HEARING on Promises Made, Promises Broken: The Impact of Chronic Underfunding of Contract Health Services, 111th Cong., 1st sess., December 3, 2009. See statement by Connie Whidden, Health Director, Seminole Tribe of Florida.

[47] U.S. Government Accountability Office, *Medicare and Medicaid: CMS and State Efforts to Interact with the Indian Health Service and Indian Tribes* , 08-724, July 11, 2008.

[48] Ibid. UIOs may charge copayments, and PPACA permits ITs and TOs to charge some copayments. See *Indian Health Care Improvement Act Provisions in the Patient Protection and Affordable Care Act (P.L. 111-148)*, by Elayne J. Heisler and Roger Walke.

[49] See CRS Report R40942, *Private Health Insurance Provisions in the Patient Protection and Affordable Care Act (PPACA)*, by Hinda Chaikind et al., for description of the exchanges.

Index

C

D

E

F

G

H

I

Q

R

S

T

U